Python for
Data Science

Deep Machine Learning Algorithms in Python and Artificial Intelligence. Crash Course to Measure Value of Big Data and Analyzes what Matters to Live by Computer Programming

Mik Arduino

Table of Contents

Introduction

Congratulations on purchasing *Python for Data Science* and thank you for doing so.

The following chapters will discuss all of the steps that you need to know in order to get started with Python for data science today. There are a lot of different parts that come with a data science project, and this guidebook is going to walk you through all of them so that you can learn how to make them work for some of your own needs. We will be able to take control of all of that data that we have been collecting and can move on from there to use that data to give us a competitive advantage overall.

The beginning of this guidebook is going to take some time to explore some of the different parts that we need to know before getting started with the data analysis. We are going to spend some time looking at a few different parts of artificial intelligence and how we are able to use this to help us to work on teaching our computer how to learn on its own. We will explore some of the basics of artificial intelligence, machine learning, and deep learning and how all three of these topics are going to come together to help us to get the most out of our computers and programming them.

After we have taken a look at some of these topics of artificial intelligence, it is time to move on to some of the things that we need to do in order to handle data science. This part is going to look at some of the steps that are needed in order to help us work with a data science project, the benefits of working with these projects for your business, and the lifecycle of data science. We will also explore what big data is all about, and why this is an important part of the whole process.

From there, it is time to work with some of the parts of a data science project, and how we are able to put all of this together to help us to see some good results in the process as well. We are going to look at the steps of cleaning and organizing our data so that it is ready to work with any algorithm that we choose. We will explore how Python can work with data analysis and helps us to pick and create some of the different algorithms that we really need, and so much more.

The end of this guidebook is going to spend some time taking a look at a lot of the different machine learning and Python algorithms that you can use in order to help complete the data analysis and tell you all of the great insights and predictions that are inside of your data. Some of the different algorithms we are going to take a look at including the KNN, clustering, Naïve Bayes, Support Vector Machines, and Markov Algorithms. And then we will finish off with some of the basics of working with a data visualization and why this is so important to some of the work that we want to do in order to understand those complex relationships in our data.

A data science project is going to be one of the best things that you can do for your business. It will help you to understand more about your industry, about your customers, about the other companies that you are competing against, and so much more. Being able to do this in an efficient and accurate manner is going to be so important to the success of what you are doing for your business. When you are ready to learn how to get started with your data science project, and you want to make sure that you are doing it the right way, make sure to check out this guidebook to help you get started

There are plenty of books on this subject on the market, thanks again for choosing this one! Every effort was made to ensure it is full of as much useful information as possible, please enjoy it!

Chapter 1: A Look at Artificial Intelligence

Artificial intelligence is going to make it possible for machines to learn from the experiences that they go through, to adjust to new inputs when necessary, and perform tasks similar to how a human can do them as well. Most examples of artificial intelligence that we are going to hear about right now, whether we are looking at a self-driving car or a computer that can play chess, are going to rely on a number of processes like natural language processing and deep learning. Using these kinds of technologies will allow our computer to be trained in order to accomplish some specific tasks, usually through processing a large amount of data and recognizing the patterns that show up in the data as well.

There is so much that we are able to do when it comes to artificial intelligence. And while some of the ideas that come with this have been around for some time, it is important for us to take a closer look at this topic and experience more about what it means, and how it can work for our business, and for a lot of the technology that we are going to use on a regular basis. Let's dive into the ideas of artificial intelligence and learn how this is going to work for our needs.

Artificial Intelligence History

The first thing that we are going to take a look at here is the history of artificial intelligence. This was a term that was first coined in 1956. But since this kind of intelligence has become more popular today thanks to the increased volumes of data, the different algorithms that are more advanced, and improvements to storage and computing power that are there, we can see why it is growing so much.

In the beginning, some of the early research that was done on this topic explored a lot of different types of topics like symbolic methods and problem-solving. Then a few years later, the US Department of Defense started to take a little closer look at this kind of work and started to use it as a way to train computers to mimic some of the basic reasoning that we find with humans. For example, there is a project done called DARPA, or Defense Advanced Research Projects, Agency, that was able to complete street mapping projects for us in the 1970s. and then this was able to take us even further in 2003 to provide us with some personal assistants, which is much before when we saw them with some of the products like Cortana and Alexa that we see and use today.

This history of artificial intelligence was able to help pave the way for some of the formal reasoning and automation that we are going to see in the computers and other products that we use on a regular basis today. We may see them in some of the products that we use like smart search systems, decision support systems, and more that are designed in order to augment and even complement some of the abilities that we see reserved for humans.

While the movies and novels about science fiction that we have seen throughout the years will depict artificial intelligence more like robots who are similar to humans and take over the world, you will find that the current evolution that comes with artificial intelligence is not that scary. Instead, it is going to be seen as pretty smart instead. Instead, artificial intelligence is going to evolve in order to provide us with many benefits in all sorts of industries all around and it is likely that the influence of artificial intelligence is going to grow and change a lot in the future as well.

Why Is Artificial Intelligence So Important?

The next thing that we need to discuss is why artificial intelligence is going to be so important. Why do we need to spend some time talking about this topic, and is it really worth our time for us to know what this is all about? There are a lot of things that artificial intelligence is going to be able to do for us, and these will include some of the following:

Artificial intelligence is able to automate some of the repetitive discovery and learning that we need to accomplish through the data that we have. but artificial intelligence is going to be quite a bit different from some of the regular automation that we will see. Instead of going through and automating manual tasks, artificial intelligence is going to perform frequent, computerized, and high-volume tasks reliably, and we will not have to worry about it getting tired and fatiguing in the process either.

Another benefit is that artificial intelligence is going to help us add some more intelligence to our existing products. We will find that when we utilize this kind of intelligence in the proper manner, we will be able to take a lot of the products that are already in existence and make them smart, and easier to work with. In most cases, we will find that this artificial intelligence is not going to be sold on its own or in individual applications.

Instead, we will find that many of the products that we are going to use and that are already on the market will see some improvements when we add in some of the capabilities of artificial intelligence, such as Siri. Automation, bots, smart machines, and some conversational platforms are going to be combined with large amounts of data in order to improve many technologies at home and in the workplace. We can see this kind of technology happen with the things that happen in our worlds such as investment analysis and security intelligence.

We will find that artificial intelligence is also able to analyze deeper and more data than we were able to do in the past, thanks to something that is known as neural networks. These neural networks are going to have a lot of hidden layers that help it to learn along the way and will help us to really find out what information and patterns are found in our data.

For example, we are now able to build up a system for fraud detection that will have five hidden layers, which is something that was pretty much impossible to do just a few years ago. All that has been changed thanks to big data and all of the computing power that we have today. Of course, we need to make sure that we have a ton of data available in order to train our models of deep learning because this is the way that they learn, straight from the data. With this one, the more data, the better when it comes to the accuracy levels you are able to get.

Artificial intelligence can also benefit us because it is going to adapt through progressive learning algorithms to let the data do some of the programmings that are needed. AI is going to find structure and some of the regularities that come with the data so that the algorithm is effectively acquiring a new skill. The algorithm, through this process, is able to become a predictor or a classifier depending on the situation that is going on.

So, just like an algorithm has the ability to teach itself the steps to playing chess, it is also able to use some of the same ideas in order to teach itself what products it should recommend to a person online. And the models are going to make the necessary adaptations when they are given some new data as well. Backpropagation is going to be a technique of AI that will ensure that the adjustment of the model happens, through training and data that is added, especially when the answer that the model is giving is not quite right.

We will also find that through the right algorithm, and plenty of training, artificial intelligence is going to be able to achieve an incredible amount of accuracy. This is thanks to the process of deep neural networks, something that has allowed us to handle a lot of projects and more that seemed impossible in the past.

With this one, we may see that some of the interactions that we do with Alexa and other similar products are based on the idea of deep learning, and they are going to get more accurate the more time that we spend with them. In the medical field, we are able to see some more examples of how this work because we will find AI techniques from deep learning, object recognition, and image classification can now be used to help find out cancer in an MRI with the same accuracy that was formerly only found in highly trained radiologists.

And finally, another reason why artificial intelligence is going to be found as important is that it is the tool that we need to get the most out of the data that we are using. When we work with a self-learning algorithm the data that we are focusing on is going to become intellectual property for that company as well. The answers are going to be in the data, we just need to use some of the processes of AI in order to get this data and these patterns out.

Since the role of this data is now playing an even bigger role in most businesses than it did in the past, it is going to provide those who use it with a big competitive advantage. If you are the company that has the best and the most data in an industry that is highly competitive, even if everyone else is working with techniques that are similar, the company with the best data is going to be the one that wins out in the end.

How Is Artificial Intelligence Being Used?

The next thing that we need to focus on here when it comes to artificial intelligence is how it is being used. It is easy enough to say that we are able to work with artificial intelligence and see that it can help a computer or a machine learn like a human, but are there actually some practical applications of using this kind of technology? Are there actually companies out there who are willing and able to use this kind of technology for their own benefits as well?

Yes, there is. In fact, pretty much every industry you can think about has a high demand for some of the capabilities that are there for artificial intelligence, especially systems that are meant to answer questions to help out with medical research, risk notification, patent searches, and legal assistance to name a few. There are a ton of other industries who are able to benefit from the use of this artificial intelligence as well, and some of the most prevalent of these will include:

The field of healthcare. Artificial intelligence and all of the applications that come with it are able to provide us with the personalized machine and X-ray readings and more. Personal health care assistants can act as life coaches to be there to help remind us to take our pills, eat healthier, and to get enough exercise. Doctors are able to use this technology to read through charts and results faster, and it can even help assist with some surgeries that need more finesse and care than others.

The world of manufacturing is going to benefit when we take a look at the idea of artificial intelligence as well. This kind of technology is going to be able to analyze the factory of IoT data as it is able to stream from the connected equipment. This can be used in order to forecast the load that is expected and the demand thanks to some recurrent networks. This can also be used to help a company figure out when a machine may go down or a part needs to be replaced so they can go through and get this fixed at a more opportune time.

The next industry that is able to benefit from the use of artificial intelligence in the field of retail. Artificial intelligence is going to provide us with a lot of shopping capabilities that are virtual and can even offer some recommendations that are personalized while discussing purchase options with the consumer. Stock management and site layout technologies are also going to see some improvements with this technology over time.

And finally, we are going to take a look at the world of banking. Artificial intelligence is going to enhance the precision, effectiveness, and speed of the efforts of a human. In the world of banking, these techniques are going to be used to help them to figure out which transactions are likely to be fraudulent. It can also help them to adopt systems of fast and accurate credit scoring, and can even automate some of the manually intense tasks that come with data management as well.

Some of the Challenges of Artificial Intelligence

We just spent some time discussing how artificial intelligence is able to change up some parts of every industry, but it is also important to understand some of the limits that come with this. The principle kind of limitation that we are going to see with this technology is that the algorithms of it are going to learn from the data. There is no other way that knowledge can go through the algorithm and be successful.

What this means for our algorithms as well as the predictions and patterns that we are working with is that if there are any inaccuracies in the data that we are sending through the algorithm, then this is going to reflect itself in the results. And any additional layers of prediction or analysis need to be gone through in a separate manner to be successful.

In addition, we will find that the systems that work with artificial intelligence right now are going to be trained to work with one clearly defined task, and they are not able to take on more than one thing at a time. this means that a system that is set up to learn how to play poker will not be able to play the game of chess or solitaire. The system that is able to help a bank out with detecting fraud is not going to be able to go through and provide you with legal advice. In fact, an AI system that is able to detect fraud in the health care industry still will not be able to detect fraud in other places like in taxes or a warranty claims the position.

What we mean by this is that these systems are great, but they are going to be incredibly specialized. They are going to focus on doing one single task really well, which means that they are going to be far from behaving in the same manner as a human. In addition, the self-learning systems that we are working with here are not going to be autonomous systems. The technologies that are imagined and used I TV and movies are still going to be part of science fiction for now.

This doesn't mean that there isn't a lot of potentials that come with using artificial intelligence. It simply means that we need to be aware that there are some limitations that come with using this kind of process and there are times when it is not going to work the best for our needs all of the time. Knowing when to work with artificial intelligence and some of the applications that come with it can provide more value to you than anything else.

How Does Artificial Intelligence Work?

Artificial intelligence is going to work in the most effective manner when we are able to combine together a large amount of data with fast, iterative processing and some intelligent algorithms. This is necessary because it is going to allow our software to have the ability to learn from features and patterns in our data in an automatic manner. This is going to be a pretty broad field of study that is going to include a bunch of technologies, methods, and theories to go along with it. Some of the major subfields that you will be able to see when it comes to using artificial intelligence will include:

1. Machine learning: This is a process that is going to automate some of the analytical model building. It is going to use some methods from operations research, statistics, neural networks, and even

physics in order to find some of the hidden insights in the data, without the programmer having to go through and explicitly program the algorithm on what to think about the data or where to look for it.

2. Neural networks: This is going to be one of the types of machine learning that is going to be made up of units that are interconnected and are able to process information. They are able to do this by responding to some of the external inputs, relaying information between each of the units. This is going to be a process that will require multiple passes at the data in order to find the connections and derive meaning from the data.

3. Deep learning: This is a type of learning that has huge neural networks that will have lots of layers to process units, taking advantage of advances in computing power and improved training techniques in order to learn some complex patterns in large amounts of data. Some of the common applications of using this would be things like speech and image recognition.

4. Cognitive computing: This is going to be one of the subfields of artificial intelligence that is going to strive, as closely as possible, for natural and

human-like interaction with the machines. Using cognitive computing with artificial intelligence, the ultimate goal is for a machine to simulate the processes of a human through the ability to interpret images and speech, and then be able to give a response that is coherent.

5. Computer vision: This is a part that will rely on pattern recognition and deep learning in order to recognize what is in a video or a picture. When machines are able to process, analyze, and understand images, they are able to capture the images or videos in real-time and then interpret the surroundings.

6. Natural language processing: This is going to give your computer the ability to analyze, understand, and then generate human language, and sometimes this even includes speech. The next stage that is going to come with this is going to include natural language interaction, which is going to allow a human to communicate with computers using normal and everyday language to get all of the tasks done.

There are also a number of different features and technologies that can come into play that will ensure that artificial intelligence is as successful as possible. For example, graphical processing units are going to be a key part of this because they will make sure that we have the heavy computing power that is needed to have iterative processing. Training the neural networks will require that the company has the right kind of big data, along with enough computing power to get it all done.

Another thing that we are able to look at when it comes to helping out artificial intelligence is the Internet of Things or IoT. This is going to be something that is able to generate a large amount of data from devices that are connected, and most of it is not going to be analyzed yet. Automating models that come with artificial intelligence will allow us to be able to use more of it.

There are also a number of advanced algorithms that we are able to use to make sure that we are going to get the most out of artificial intelligence. These advanced algorithms are always being developed and then combined together in a new way to help us to analyze the data we have faster and at multiple levels. This kind of processing is going to be key to identifying and predicting some rare events, understanding some of the complex systems, and optimizing some unique scenarios as well.

And finally, we will see that application processing interfaces, or APIs, are going to be useful as well. These are going to be packages of code that are portable that will make it possible to ad din some AI functionality to the existing products and software packages. They are also going to be able to add in some image recognition capabilities to things like home security systems, and even the capabilities of Q&A to help describe data, make headlines and captions, or call out some of the interesting insights and patterns that are found in our data.

We have spent quite a bit of time in this chapter takes a look at artificial intelligence and all of the different parts that are going to come with it. There is a lot that we are able to explore with this idea and topic, and so much more that we can still look through as we progress through this guidebook. You will find that with the ideas of artificial intelligence, knowing the basics will just scratch the surface, and it is likely that as time goes on, we are going to find more and more uses of this technology as well.

Chapter 2: What Is Machine Learning?

Now that we have had some time to look over some of the parts that we need to know when it comes to artificial intelligence, it is now time for us to move on and learn a bit more about machine learning and what this process is able to do for us. There is a lot that we are able to benefit from when it comes to working with machine learning, and it is important to note that while it is going to sound like a similar approach as artificial intelligence, it is actually going to be something quite different.

Sometimes the big confusion that shows up between artificial intelligence and machine learning comes from the fact that machine learning is a type of artificial intelligence. This machine learning is going to be one of the topics that fit under the umbrella of artificial intelligence, which means that it is going to be used quite often here, but we have to remember that they are both two different topics and that we are going to use them in two different manners.

With this in mind, let's dive in and look some more at some of the specifics that come with machine learning, see how it is unique on its own as a type of artificial intelligence, and why we would want to be able to work with it and the algorithms that come with it in the first place.

What Is Machine Learning?

The first part of this process that we need to take a look at is what machine learning is all about. Machine learning is basically the process that we are going to use in order to get our computers and our systems to learn how to program themselves. If the programming is automatic, then machine learning is going to be automating the process of automation.

Writing software is going to be part of the bottleneck that we are going to see here. Right now we find that there are not enough good developers out there to get the work to happen. This is then going to switch over to the idea of letting the data do all of the work, rather than waiting around for more developers to come and do it. Machine learning is one of the methods that we are able to use in order to make this happen and to make sure that programming can be scalable over time.

The best way to look at this is to do a quick comparison of traditional programming and machine learning.

Traditional programming is going to happen when the data and the program will be run on our computer and then they will produce for us an output of some kind. But with machine learning, the data and the output are going to be run on our chosen computer in order to create a program. Then this program can be used by some kind of traditional programming if needed.

Machine learning is going to be similar to gardening or farming. Seeds will be the algorithms that you use, nutrients will be the data that we provide to our data, the gardener is going to be you, and we can finish out with the plants being the programs that you are creating.

Applications of Machine Learning

There are already so many different parts that we are going to see come into play when we are working with machine learning. And as time goes on and more and more companies start to jump on board with using some of this technology for their own needs, it is likely that some of the applications are going to increase. Some of the sample applications that we are seeing with machine learning already are going to include:

1. Web search: We are able to use machine learning and some of the algorithms that come with it in order to rank a page based on what you are most likely to click on based on the searches that you do and what you clicked on in the past.

2. Computational biology: This is the process of rational design drugs in the computer-based on the experiments that were done in the past.

3. Finance: This is where we will use machine learning in order to decide which people to send out credit card offers too. It can even evaluate the risk on some of these offers and decide on where to invest money. Some financial institutions will even use this as a way to detect whether there is fraud going on with any transactions.

4. E-commerce: This is going to be used in order to help predict the customer churn that is going on. It can also be used to figure out whether or not a transaction is fraudulent at the time or not.

5. Space exploration: While this is a relatively new area of machine learning, it is possible that we are able to use some of the algorithms that come with this in order to work with space probes and radio astronomy to name a few options.

6. Robotics: We are able to work with machine learning in order to help out with some of the fields of robotics if we would like. This is going to be used in order to help us learn how to handle some of the uncertainty that can show up in new environments and can work with the self-driving car as well.

7. Information extraction: This is going to be when we use machine learning to ask questions over a database, no matter where it is found throughout the web.

8. Social networks; This is where we will use machine learning in order to check on some of the relationships and the preferences that show up in the data. Machine learning is especially going to be used here to extract some of the patterns and the value that come out of that data.

9. Debugging: This is where we will use computer science problems to help us to debug our programs and computers. It could also help to limit the amount of work that is found in a labor-intensive process. It is even used to help us suggest where the bug could be.

As we can see, there are already a ton of different applications where we are going to see the use of machine learning on a regular basis. Being able to keep this under control and learning where we would be able to benefit from this kind of technology the most is going to be a critical step to ensuring that we are going to get the most out of machine learning and that we will actually be able to use it for some of our needs.

The good news is that no matter what industry you are in, or how you serve your customers, there is a spot for machine learning with your business. You may have to experiment with this one a bit to learn some of the different ways that we are able to work with this kind of thing, but you will need to make sure that you look at all of the options to see just how amazing this process can be.

The Key Elements of Machine Learning

Now that we have been able to learn a little bit more about machine learning and some of the ways that we are able to use this kind of learning for our own needs, it is time to look at a few of the major elements that are going to come with this kind of learning. There are tens of thousands of machine learning algorithms that you are able to work with, and because of the popularity that these have right now with so many businesses, you can see why there are so many new algorithms that are being developed all of the time.

All of these algorithms are there to help you out, but you may find that working with these is going to be a bit confusing overall if you are not careful. You want to make sure that you understand what is going on with the algorithms and how you are able to use them for some of your own needs. The good news is that each of these algorithms is going to have three main components that they will share in common, and these are going to include:

1. Representation: This means that they are going to have a way to represent knowledge. These could include options like model ensembles, support vector machines, neural networks, graphical models, instances, sets of rules, and decision trees to name a few.

2. Evaluation: This means that they need to have a way to evaluate your hypotheses or candidate programs. Some of the examples that you will see

with this one will include margin, cost, posterior probability, likelihood, squared error, recall, prediction, and accuracy.

3. Optimization: This is going to be the way that the candidate programs are going to be generated and it can be known as the search process in some cases. For example, you may find that these work with constrained optimization, convex optimization, and combinatorial optimization.

All of the different machine learning algorithms that we have and can choose from are going to have a combination of these three components in place before they even get started. this is one of the best kinds of frameworks that you are able to use in order to gain a good understanding of all algorithms.

Different Types of Machine Learning

One thing that you will notice pretty quickly when you are working with machine learning is that there will be four types of machine learning that we need to focus on. These are going to include supervised, semi-supervised unsupervised, and reinforcement learning. Let's take a look at how these are all going to work and why they are all important to some of the work that we want to do within machine learning.

To start is the supervised machine learning. This is where we are going to train our algorithms with the input, as well as the corresponding output, that we want it to have. This allows the algorithm to have a bunch of examples of what it should know before you even start, and can make it easier to get the results that you want in the process as well. This is where we would like to have an input and we know what the desired output is all about. For example, we could have a piece of equipment that could have some data points that are labeled R for runs or F for failed. The learning algorithm is going to be able to get a set of inputs along with the corresponding correct outputs, and then the algorithm is able to learn when they compare the actual output with the right outputs to see if there are errors present.

From here, it is then going to be able to make some modifications to the model as well. Through methods like classification, prediction, and regression, as well as gradient boosting, this kind of learning is going to help us use patterns to predict the values of a label on additional unlabeled data. This kind of learning is going to be used in a lot of applications where we want to take some historical data and then use it to make some predictions about what is going to happen in the future. For example, we are able to use this kind of learning in order to help us better figure out when a credit card transaction is going to be seen as fraudulent, or when one of the customers of an insurance company is most likely to file a claim against them.

Then there is going to be the type of learning that is known as semi-supervised learning. This is going to be pretty similar to both the supervised machine learning and unsupervised machine learning because it is going to use a combination of the two ideas. With this one, we are going to use a little bit of labeled data, with a lot of unlabeled data, in order to train the algorithm to behave in the manner that we want.

The reason for this is because labeled data is expensive. It may be the most effective to get the work done and can help us to see some great results with what we are doing in the process. But it is time-consuming and expensive to find all of the labeled data that we need. This kind of algorithm can be a good compromise because it allows us a chance to find the data that we want while ensuring that we will get the algorithm trained as efficiently as possible.

The next type of algorithm that we are able to work with here is going to be the unsupervised machine learning algorithm. This one is going to be a good one to choose when we would like to work with analyzing data that doesn't have any labels on it or any help identifying it in the first place. The system is not going to be told the right answer from the beginning, which is kind of the opposite of what we see with supervised learning. Instead, it is going to be up to the algorithm to take a look at the data and figure out what is there and what patterns it needs to share.

The goal here is for the algorithm to explore the data and see if it is able to find some structure inside of it. Unsupervised learning is going to work well when we want to handle some of our transactional data. For example, it can help us to identify some segments of our customers with similar attributes who can then be treated in a similar manner with our marketing campaigns.

Or we are able to work with these algorithms in order to help us figure out the main attributes that are going to help us to segment out our customers from one another. There are a lot of different types of algorithms that we are able to use when we want to focus on unsupervised machine learning. Some of these techniques are going to include self-organizing maps, nearest-neighbor mapping, k-means clustering, and more. These are also the same kinds of algorithms that we are able to do when it comes to segmenting out the text topics, identify the outliers that are in the data, and even recommend items on a website as well if needed.

And then we are going to move through and take a look at the idea of reinforcement machine learning. This is going to be a bit different than unsupervised machine learning, through to someone who is just starting out, it is going to appear to have a lot of similarities to the other option. This one is going to rely more on the idea of trial and error in order to learn though and will strive to take the course that will provide it with the biggest reward in the end. When the system isn't able to get a good reward, it knows that this is not the path to take, and so it will take a different one the next time.

With the idea of reinforcement learning, we are going to see that there are three main components that are going to show up. We are going to start with an agent, who will be the decision-maker or the learner for the work we are doing. Then we will move on to the environment, which is going to include each of the parts of this process that the agent is able to interact with. And then we will end with the third component, which is the actions, or any of the things that our agent is able to do.

The objective here is for the agent to go through and work with actions that will maximize the expected reward over time, and not just at that time period. The agent will be able to learn as they do this that they can reach the goal much faster when they follow a good policy, based on the conditions that are set up. So the goal with this kind of learning, when compared to some of the other types, is to learn the best policy and then stick with it.

All four of these options will be important when it comes to helping us to work with machine learning and will ensure that we are going to be able to get the right algorithm in place based on the kind of data that we are focusing on at the time. Learning how to work with each of these types is going to be critical to ensuring that we are going to be able to actually use machine learning in the manner that we would like.

The Need for Machine Learning

Ever since the technical revolution, we have been able to generate a large amount of data. So much so, that it is almost impossible for us to measure how much there is. Since we have all of this data already, it is finally possible for companies in all industries to go through and build up some predictive models that are able to study, and then analyze, this complex data in the hopes of finding useful insights and to deliver results that are more accurate than before.

In fact, this is becoming such a big thing that some of the top tier companies in the world, including Amazon and Netflix to name a few, are going to build up their own models of machine learning by using a ton of data. This allows them to avoid some of the unwanted risks that no business wants to deal with and to find the more profitable opportunities that are out there.

As you dive into all of the different parts of machine learning and what it entails, you will find a whole bunch of reasons why this is so important. But some of the biggest reasons why machine learning is going to be so important will include the following:

1. It is able to handle the increase in data generation. Due to the excessive production of data, we need a method that can be used in order to structure, analyze, and then draw some useful insights from data. This is where the idea of machine learning is going to come in. it is going to be able to use data to solve problems and find solutions to some of the biggest tasks that are faced by organizations.

2. Improve the decision-making process. Thanks to the fact that we are able to make sure of a lot of different algorithms, we can use machine learning to help us make some better business decisions. It can help companies to identify some of the anomalies that they are going to face, identify the biggest risks to themselves, predict when the stock market is going to fall, and even forecast sales.

3. To help uncover patterns and trends that are found in your data. Finding these hidden patterns and

then extracting some of the key patterns from this data is going to be one of the most essential parts of machine learning. By building predictive models and using statistical techniques machine learning allows us to dig beneath the surface and explore the data at a smaller scale. Understanding this data and extracting patterns manually will take a long time but the algorithms with machine learning will be able to get all of this done in a few seconds.

4. It can solve some complex problems. Machine learning can help us out with a lot of different problems, including things like building cars that can drive themselves to detect genes that are linked to diseases.

There are a lot of companies out there right now who are willing and already using machine learning and all that it has to offer. The first example of this is the recommendation engine form Netflix. The core of this whole program is its recommendation engine. Over 75 percent of what people watch on this streaming service is going to be something that Netflix recommends, and these recommendations are done thanks to the use of machine learning.

Another way that machine learning is being used is with the auto-tagging feature on Facebook. The logic behind the face verification that we see on Facebook is going to be all about neural networks and machine learning. The process of DeepMind, which helps Facebook do this process, is that it studies the facial features in an image before tagging your family and friends in it.

Amazon uses machine learning in a number of manners, but the Alexa product is one of the most well-known. This product is going to be based on machine learning and natural language processing to help provide us with an advanced level virtual assistant that is able to do a lot of work for you. This is going to ensure that we are able to get the best results out of this process and that the device will be able to work the way that we need.

And then there is the spam filter that comes with Google. Gmail is already making sure of machine learning and other tools in order to sort out the many spam messages that you get on a regular basis. It is going to rely on machine learning algorithms and natural language processing in order to analyze the emails it receives in real-time and then it can classify these as either spam or non-spam based on what it thinks.

Of course, these are just a few examples that we are going to find when it is time to work with machine learning. There are many businesses out there who have started to work with machine learning and all of the different parts that come with it, and it is important that we learn the right steps to make all of this happen for our needs as well. If your business is looking into using machine learning, look at all of the cool ways that you can already use it for your needs.

Chapter 3: Taking It Deep with Deep Machine Learning

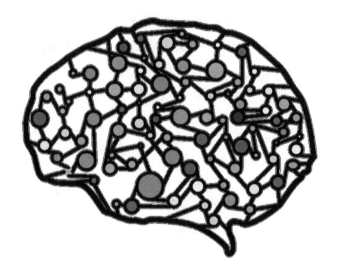

We started with an introduction to artificial intelligence and what that is able to do for some of the work that we see with machine learning. And now it is time to take all of that a little bit further and move on to another form of machine learning known as deep machine learning, or deep learning. This is slightly different than what we saw before when we were just working with machine learning, but it is still going to have an important point in the whole process. Let's dive in and see what we can do with the help of deep machine learning.

What Is Deep Learning?

To start with here, we need to take a closer look at what deep learning is all about. Deep learning is going to be a function of artificial intelligence that is able to imitate how we see the human brain function and work, at least when it comes to processing data and creating patterns that we can then use to make some smart decisions for our business. Deep learning is also going to be seen as a subset of machine learning within the artificial intelligence, which is going to have networks that are capable of learning unsupervised from the data that it receives, even if that data is not structured or it is unlabeled. In some cases, this kind of learning is going to be known as a deep neural network or deep neural learning as well.

So, how does this deep learning really work? Deep learning has evolved so much in the past few years, and we see it growing along with the growth of the digital era. This digital era has been huge because it has brought along with it a huge explosion of data in all forms, and from all parts of the world as well. This data, which we are going to call big data, is going to be drawn from a variety of sources including search engines, e-commerce platforms if you have one, social media, and online cinemas to name a few.

Pretty much anywhere can provide us with the data that we want. It is often more of a fact of what kind of data we are looking for to help out with the analysis, how much of the data we would like to work with, and what we are going to use the data for in the first place. With all of the data that is out there and readily available to us, we can easily find the information, we then need to figure out how to use it. This enormous amount of data is going to be easy to access and we are able to share and use it in any manner that we would like through options like cloud computing.

However, the data, which is normally going to be unstructured, is so vast that it could take decades or more before a human would be able to go through it and really understand what it is saying. There is just so much of it that it is hard to think about going through it manually and finding out what is inside of it. Companies realize that there is a lot of potentials that are found in this data, and they still want to get through it all, even though it is impractical to allow a human to do this work. This is why many of these companies are adopting systems from AI in order to provide them with some of the automated support to help with this.

Machine Learning vs. Deep Learning

In the past section, we spent some time taking a look at machine learning and what it is all about. So naturally, it is going to seem like there are a lot of similarities that we are going to see between the topic of machine learning that we were talking about and the topic of deep learning that we are exploring a little bit more now. We want to know how they are similar and how there are differences between the two along the way.

One of the most common techniques that we are going to see when it is time to process this big data is going to be machine learning. This is going to include an algorithm that is self-adaptive and that is going to get better and better at analysis and providing us with patterns with more experience over time or when we are able to add in some data to the mix that is new.

So, let's say that if a digital payments company is looking through its records and would like to figure out the potential or the occurrence of fraud in the system, it could use the different tools of machine learning to help out with this purpose. The computational algorithm that was built into your chosen computer model is going to process all of the transactions that are happening on the digital platform, then will find patterns in the data before setting out to tell us where any of the anomalies in this pattern are going to show up.

Now we will find that deep learning is going to be a kind of subset to machine learning. This is going to utilize a more hierarchical level of these networks in order to help us to carry out some of the purposes that come with machine learning. The artificial neural networks are going to be built in a similar manner to the human brain.

This means that the neuron nodes are going to be connected together like a web.

While some of the traditional programs are going to build up an analysis with the data in a more linear manner, the hierarchical function of deep learning is going to allow for a machine to process data with a more nonlinear approach, which can save a lot of time and effort in the process.

Going back to our idea of the fraud approach, we will find that the traditional methods of handling this might rely more on the amount of a transaction that goes on. This may seem to make sense, but there are cases of fraud that will involve smaller amounts of money as well. With deep learning though, we are able to rely more on a nonlinear technique that would rely on a few different factors. These could look at the type of retailer, IP address, geographic location, time, and more to see whether there is fraud going on.

For example, if the person lives in Nebraska and made a purchase at 10:15 in the morning at a Walmart that they usually frequent, then this is not going to be seen as a big deal by the computer, even if it may be a slightly larger purchase. But, if that same card is then used at

10:30 in London, England, even if it is just for $50, this is going to send up an alert. Those are too close together, and the person is never in that country, so this is a sign that fraud is occurring.

The first layer of the neural network process is going to be raw data input, like how many transactions are going on, and then will pass it on to the next layer as an output. The second layer is going to process the information of the previous layer by including some additional information like the IP address of the user and then will pass on these as the results as well.

We can keep going through these layers, with the following layer taking on the information of the second layer and including some more raw data that is needed, like the geographic location, which is going to make the patterns that the machine is finding even better. This is going to continue on through all of the different levels of this network that we have created until the algorithm is able to tell us, with pretty good certainty, that the transaction is either fraudulent or not.

Keep in mind during this process that deep learning is going to be a function of artificial intelligence that is able to mimic the workings of the human brain when it is time to process data to use in your decision-making process. Deep learning in this process is going to be able to learn from data that is unlabeled and unstructured, so it will do well with unsupervised machine learning as well. Deep learning, as a subset of machine learning, is able to help us out with a bunch of different options, including helping financial institutions figure out whether fraud or money laundering is going on with them.

More About Deep Learning

It is best if we are able to take a look at deep learning from a more laymen kind of terms to make it easier. In general, we are going to focus on two tasks at a time and we will do these consciously or subconsciously based on what kind of information we are working with. This could be the idea of categorization to figure out what we are able to feel through the senses earlier. And then we can have a prediction as well, which is going to be when we are going to make a prediction about the future of something based on the previous data that we have.

For example, maybe we have a hot cup of water or coffee. We are able to categorize this in the first step because we can actually feel that the cup of coffee is hot at that time when we are holding onto it. This is a pretty simple idea. But then we are going to use the idea of prediction to figure out how the coffee is going to be in the future. If we do nothing to the cup of coffee, then this is a sign that we are going to have cold coffee the more time that goes on.

We are going to be able to use the idea of categorization and prediction for tasks on more than one event, and some of the examples of how we are going to see this happen in our daily lives will include:

1. Holding onto a cup that has some kind of liquid in it. We are able to figure out whether it is hot or cold and will be this way in the future.
2. Email categorization such as whether that email is spam or not spam.
3. Daylight time categorization such as figuring out whether it is night or day outside.
4. Being able to make some long-term plans for the future. These are usually going to be based on where we are right now, the things that we have, and how we think things are going to stay the same or change in the future. This is going to be known as the prediction.

You will find that all creatures throughout the world are going to be able to do some of these tasks in their life. For example, animals will crow in order to figure out the best place to build their nest, and a bee is going to use some other factors about when and where to get honey. Humans are going to use this to figure out a lot of the things that they want to know in their daily lives as well.

Now that we know a little bit more about these ideas of categorization and prediction, it is important for us to move on to a bit about how we would like to use them in an image. For categorization, we are going to take a look at how we are able to set up a program that is able to categorize between dogs and cats, simply by drawing a line that goes through the points of data, and then when we are doing this with the lens of prediction, we are instead going to draw a line through the points of data to help us make some good predictions of when things will increase and decrease.

The first part we are going to take a look at here will be the categorization. There are going to be a few things that need to come into play when we are doing this though. In general, when we are trying to categorize between dogs and cats, or something else, we are not going to draw up a line in our brains, and the position of the cats and dogs will be pretty arbitrary for illustration purposes only. We can imagine that being able to do this kind of categorization is going to be more complex than just drawing a line as well.

We are going to spend our time working on doing a categorization between two things that are based on what they look like, their height, size, and shapes, and sometimes it is going to be more difficult in order to do this based on the features of maybe a small dog that is fury and comparing it to a new-born cat. This is going to show us that there is not really a clear-cut categorization that we can use. It takes a lot of trial and error to make all of this happen.

Once we are able to categorize between dogs and cats when we are young children and then as we grow into adults, it becomes easier for us to go through and do this kind of categorization on any cat or dog, even if it is one that we have not seen in the past.

Then we are able to move on to working with prediction. For prediction that is based on a line, we are going to spend some time drawing through these points of data, if we are first able to go through and predict where it is most likely to go either up or down. The curve is also going to help us make a prediction of fitting the new points of data within the range of existing points of data. This could include looking at things based on how close the new point of data is to the curve.

Another thing that we need to look at with prediction is which of the points of data are that appear red in color and which ones will be within and past the range of the existing points of data, and the curve is going to attempt to predict both of these.

As we can see, we are going to often end up with a good and similar endpoint with both the prediction and the categorization. If we are then able to train the computer model that we are working with to draw the curvy line based on the points of data when we are done, then we are going to be able to extend this out to apply to a bunch of different models, such as drawing a curvy line in a 3D plane and more. These are all things that we are able to work with when we spend our time training a deep learning model with a lot of labeled and unlabeled data along the way.

Example of Deep Learning

The next thing that we need to take a look at is an example of deep learning. We can go back to the detection system for fraud that we talked about before and how this is going to work with machine learning. When we use this example, it is easier for us to create our own example of deep learning. If a system of machine learning is able to create a model with parameters built around a number of dollars that a user is going to receive and send, then the method of deep learning can start building on the kinds of results that this machine learning system is going to provide to us.

Each layer that we are going to see with our neural networks will be unique, and they will be able to build upon the layer that came with it, with any of the added data that we want. Some of this added data could include things like IP address, credit score, event on social media, user, sender retailer, and other key features that are going to help us to see what is going on with the payments and more, but which would take years for a human to go through and actually figure out on their own.

The algorithms that you are going to be able to use with deep learning have been trained to not just be able to create patterns from all of the transactions, but also to know when a pattern is signaling the need for an investigation because it looks like something fraudulent is happening. The final layer of the neural network is going to be able to relay a signal up to one of the analysts who are able to freeze the account for the user until there is time to do an investigation into the process and see what is going on.

Deep learning, as we can imagine, is going to be used in order to help all sorts of industries and can be used to help out with a number of different tasks. Commercial apps that are going to rely on some of the work of image recognition, open-source platforms that are going to help to provide recommendations to the consumer, and some of the medical research tools that are going to be able to explore the possibility of taking a common drug and using it on a new ailment are all going to be examples of what we are able to do when we incorporate deep learning into the work that we do.

Chapter 4: How This All Fits Into Data Science

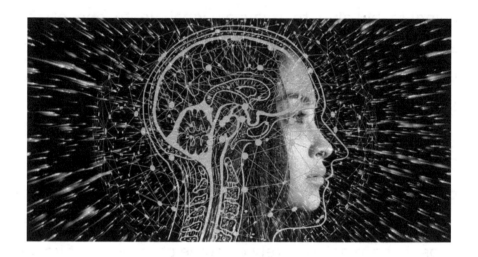

So far in this guidebook, we have spent some time taking a look at some of the basics of artificial intelligence, machine learning, and deep learning. All of these are really important terms that we need to spend some of our time and attention on because they will help us to create some of the algorithms and more that we need to handle some of the work that we are going to do with data science. We are going to spend some time looking at data science in this chapter, and you will find how all of the three topics from above are going to be able to fit into the same kind of idea along the way.

As the world started to enter into the era of big data more than ever before, the need to learn how to use this data and how to store it also grew. This was going to be one of the biggest challenges and concerns for a lot of businesses until about 2010. The main focus was then on building solutions and frameworks to store all of this data. Now when some of the needed frameworks were brought out and used to help solve this problem, all of this focus then shifted to the processing of all this data.

And this is where data science is going to come into play to make things easier. There is so much data out there that we need to spend our time focusing on, and it is pretty much impossible for us to really learn from this data in a manual manner. Instead, we need to use data science, combined with machine learning and deep learning algorithms, in order to sort through the data that we have and putting it all together to work the way that we need.

Why Do I Need Data Science?

The first thing that we need to take a look at with this process is why I need to work with data science. In the traditional way of business, the data that was available to businesses was going to come to them in a structured form, and it was going to be pretty small in size. This was going to make it easier to analyze with some of the simple business intelligence tools that were around at the time. This was easier to learn from and use the way that we would like.

But things have changed, and there is now so much more that we are able to look through when it comes to data. This is exciting for a lot of businesses because it opens up a lot of doors for them. But it also brings up some unique challenges when it is time to actually sort through all of the data. Unlike some of the data that we saw in those older and traditional systems, which often came to us in a more structured format, today most of the data that we see is going to be unstructured. Or at least semi-structured. In fact, it is estimated that by 2020, at least 80 percent of the data that is available for companies to use will be unstructured in format.

The data that businesses are using is often going to be generated form a lot of different sources including text files, financial logs, sensors, instruments, and multimedia forms. Some of the business intelligence tools that were used in the past are not able to handle all of this complex data, and this is why we need tools that are more advanced, and more algorithms, in order to analyze and draw some meaningful information out of all that data.

Of course, this is just the start of what we are able to do with data science. There are a lot of other reasons that businesses are jumping onto the process and hoping that they are able to use it for some of their needs as well. For example, how would it be to your business if you were able to understand the precise requirements of your current and future customers just by looking at the existing data that you have on the customer including their income, age, purchase history, and their past browsing history?

No doubt that this is data that your company had access to in the past. But thanks to all of the types and amounts of data, it is possible to train up the models a bit more effectively than you were able to do in the past, and now you can recommend some products to your customers with more precision than you could before. Think about how much more business this is going to bring to your company if you do it in the right manner.

And this is just the start. How would it be if you had a car that already had the intelligence that was needed to drive you home? There are already some examples of this kind of car, and it is designed in order to help collect live data from the sensors on it, including radars, lasers, and cameras in order to create a good map of what is all around it. Based on the data that is collected through here, the car is going to be able to take some decisions like when it should go faster, when to slow down, when to make a turn, and more. And all of this is going to be done with some of those machine learning algorithms that we talked about before.

We can even take a look at how to work with data science to help with predictive analytics. We are able to use this when working on a weather forecast. Data from radars, satellites, aircraft, and ships can be collected, and then we are able to do some analysis in order to build up some models. These models are not only going to be used to help us to forecast what the weather is going to do but can also help when it is time to predict any big natural calamities that are going to happen as well.

What Is Data Science

You will find that the use of data science is going to be increasingly common as more companies try to jump on and see how they are able to use this for some of their own benefits as well. But we need to take a look at what data science is all about. Remember here that data science is going to be a blend of different principles of machine learning, algorithms, and other tools in order to help us to figure out what hidden patterns are found in some of the raw data that we are working with.

We will find that a data analyst is going to spend their time explaining what is going on when they are able to process the history of the data. But a data scientist is not going to spend their time doing any exploratory analysis in order to discover insights but will work with some of the more advanced algorithms that come with machine learning in order to figure out how likely a particular event is going to happen in the future.

So, to keep it easy, a data science project is going to be used in most cases in order to make some decisions and predictions making use of a few options including machine learning, prescriptive analytics, and predictive causal analytics. Let's take a look at what each of these means and how we are able to use them.

The first one is going to be predictive causal analytics. If you would like to work with a model that is able to give you a good prediction of how possible it is that an event is going to happen sometime in the future, you need to be able to use this part of data science. Let's say that you want to provide someone with some money on credit. You also want to know how likely it is that this customer is going to make some of their future payments on time so that you get your money back. You would be able to use this part of data science in order to build up a model that is able to do an analysis of the customer payment history and use this to make a prediction on whether or not they will make their future payments on time or not.

Then we are able to move on to what is known as prescriptive analytics. If you would like to make a new model that has its own intelligence and can make some of its own decisions and can modify itself with some dynamic parameters, then it is time to work with prescriptive analytics. This is a newer field that comes with data science, but it is going to be useful because it can provide us with a lot of advice along the way as well.

The best example that we are going to see with this is the self-driving car that we heard about from Google already. The data that is gathered by vehicles can be used in order to train one of these self-driving cars. You are able to run algorithms on this data in order to make sure there is some intelligence that is brought to the whole thing. This is going to make it easier for your car to take on decisions like when to turn, which path it should take, and so much more.

Then there are also going to be a few ways that machine learning is going to come into the mix and help us out.

first, we can use machine learning to help us make some predictions. If you have a lot of transactional kind of data, such as for a financial company, and you would like to use this information in order to build up one of your own models to determine a trend in the future, then the algorithms from machine learning will be some of the best to get all of this done.

This kind of learning is going to be known as supervised learning. It is called supervised because you are already going to have the kind of data that you need based on which you are able to train your machines. For example, a model of fraud detection can be trained using some historical records of purchases that were fraudulent in the past.

And we are able to use machine learning to help us out with some pattern discovery. If you don't have the parameters based on which you are able to make predictions, then you need to go through and find out some of the hidden patterns that are inside of your set of data. This will ensure that you are able to make some predictions that are meaningful. This is nothing but unsupervised learning as you will not need to go through any predefined labels to help with the grouping. There are a few options that you can make for doing this kind of discovery of the patterns, but one of the most common of these will be clustering.

There are a lot of ways that we are able to use this, but we can say that we are working for a telephone company and it is our job to figure out where to put one or two new towers that will help benefit the customers the most. You would be able to use a technique of clustering here in order to figure out the best location for these towards ensuring in the same process that all of your users get the best signal strength possible.

Data Science vs. Business Intelligence

We have already brought up the term of business intelligence a bit in this chapter, but now we need to spend some time taking a look at what this business intelligence is all about, and why it is so important to some of the work that we are doing with this. We need to take a look at what this is and how it is going to compare to some of the neat things that we are able to do with data science.

Business intelligence is going to be able to analyze some of the previous data that you have in order to find some hindsight and some insight that allows us to describe the business trends that we are seeing. This BI is going to enable us to take the data that we have from both internal and external kinds of sources, prepare it, run queries on it, and then create dashboards that are going to help us to answer some of the questions that we have. this is also something that we are able to use to do an evaluation of the impact of certain events in the near future.

Then we have something that is known as data science. This is going to be a more forward-looking approach and an exploratory way for us to focus on analyzing the current or the past data that we have. We can then use this to predict the future outcomes with the aim of making decisions that are more informed it is going to answer some of the more open-ended questions that we have such as the what and how events are going to occur.

The Data Science Lifecycle

The next thing that we need to take a look at in order to get the most out of data science and all that it is able to offer to us is to take a look at the different steps that are going to come with this kind of process. There are a number of steps, and they can get pretty in-depth if you are not careful, but we are going to just take a look at some of the basics to help us understand what is going on and how we are able to utilize the process of data science.

To start, we have the discovery phase. Before you get very far in the project that you are working with, it is important for us to have a good understanding of what needs to go on with this process. We need to understand the various specifications, requirements, budget, and priorities that need to come into play when we are doing one of these projects.

In this step, we are going to assess whether or not we have the necessary resources in order to help get things done. We need to look to see if we have the time, the data, the people, and the technology that is needed in order to help support all of the parts of this project. In this phase, we need to frame the business problem that we want to work on, and then formulate the hypothesis that we want to use to make this happen.

This first phase is going to be a lot of information gathering and more. It is not going to really get us far into the process, but it makes sure that we know what kind of path we need to follow throughout. We know what we are working on and what we need to look for inside of our data. It is going to help us to figure out whether we have the resources that are needed or if we are able to get these resources, and more.

Once we have all of that in place, it is time for us to work on the phase that is known as data preparation. This is the phase where we are going to need to actually go through some of the data that we have collected and then figure out what is found in it, and get it prepared for some of the algorithms that we are going to use later on. IN this phase, you will need to have something known as an analytical sandbox.

This part is important because you will need to perform the analytics in it for the entire time that you plan to do the project. This is helpful because it is going to allow you a place to try things out and make sure that you can explore, preprocess, and condition the data in the proper manner before you have to go through and push it through the algorithm that you would like to use.

There are a lot of great algorithms out there that are available when it comes to data science, but we have to remember that they require the data to be higher in quality, they need the data to be organized, and all of the missing values and outliers have to be dealt with ahead of time before you try to put the information in, or you are going to end up with some inaccurate results that are not very good. You have to go through and actually work on the data that you have and make sure that it is as organized and clean as possible, to ensure that it is going to work the way that you want.

During this process, there are a number of options for coding language that you will be able to use. For the most part, companies like to work with the Python language because it is easy to learn how to use, there is a lot of power that comes behind it, and it is able to get the work done for you without a lot of struggling to learn it. Add in that there are some easy to learn variables and elements to the mix, and some of the best data science libraries are attached to the Python language, and you can see why there are so many people who want to work with this language when handling these kinds of algorithms.

The next step that we need to work with is going to be known as model planning. It is in this phase where we are going to figure out the methods, techniques, and more that we would like to use in order to draw out the patterns and any of the other relationships that are supposed to show up between the variables that we are focusing on.

Remember though this process that these relationships are going to set the base for any and all of the algorithms that you would like to work with later, in the phases that are yet to come. There are a lot of different algorithms that you are able to choose to focus on as we go through all of this, and many of them can seem flashy and really great to work with. Knowing your data, your business problem, and what you would like to get out of this whole process is going to be imperative if you would like to see the results in the end.

Once you have taken the time to plan out the model that you would like to use, it is time for us to move onto the process of building up the model that we would like to use. This is going to take some time because we need to make sure that the model is set up and ready to go while training it at the same time. IN this phase, we are going to separate out our information into two different sets. We are going to have one set that is for training our model, and one for testing our data. This is going to ensure that we are able to get the model to learn the proper way.

With the first set of data, we are going to train the algorithm on how to behave. We want to make sure that this set of data is bigger than what we are going to see with the testing dataset. This is going to ensure that the algorithm is going to be fed a ton of information on how to behave, and it will be able to learn well. The more data that you are able to provide to the algorithm during this phase, and the more accurate and the more quality that comes with this information, the better.

Then we are going to have the set of data that is used to train how well the algorithm has been able to learn along the way. This set of data is going to be a bit smaller, but it is still going to have a significant amount of data that will allow us to figure out whether the algorithm is accurate and will give us some results that we are able to trust and rely on.

During this time, we also need to consider whether some of the tools that we already have available are going to suffice for running some of the models, or if it will be better for us to have a more robust environment, such as processing that is a bit better. You will also need to analyze some of the different types of machine learning techniques that are needed, including clustering, association, and classification to figure out which one is going to help you to build up your model properly.

Then we need to spend some time looking at the steps that are needed to operationalize. In this phase of the process, you are going to deliver your final reports, briefings, code, and any of the technical documents you have to the people who need them. Usually, the data scientist is going to be someone who works for the company, someone who has the technical knowledge to help create the right machine learning algorithms and keep things moving along nicely without too much trouble along the way.

But these data scientists are usually not the ones who are going to take the results and use those to make some important decisions for the business. This will be someone else in the company. This is why the data scientist needs to be able to take down the results and the data that they got through this process, and put it into a form that is usable by someone else who may not have all of the technical knowledge that is needed for this project.

In addition, out of the first results that we are able to see with these algorithms, we may see that a pilot project is going to get started. This is a nice thing to try out if it is possible for your business because it allows us to try out some of the results that we see, on a small scale, to see how they will do in a real-time production environment. Whether it goes well or not, it is going to provide us with a clear picture of the performance and some of the other related constraints that can come upon a small scale before we go through and try to do this on a full scale.

If things do not go well after the trial period, then the project is dropped and it doesn't cost the company all that much money in the first place. However, if the project does go well, the company can see this before spending a lot of money and can make some smart decisions about whether they will proceed with implementing it throughout the whole business, or if it will just be implemented in certain areas of the business.

And finally, we need to take some time in the data science project to communicate the results. It is important for us to go through and communicate the results that were found in the algorithms and in order places with those who would use them the most. This allows us to evaluate whether the original goal was achieved or not from that first phase.

In this phase, we need to go through and identify all of the findings that were key, communicate to the right people these findings, and then determine whether or not the results that we were able to get form this project were a failure or a success. Being able to determine this is going to be based on the criteria that we took the time to form in the first phase.

Now, during this phase, there are a number of steps that we need to take in order to get started with the process. One of the best ways to help communicate some of the results that we are able to get with data science will be with visuals. The human mind is able to learn a lot more through visuals like graphs and charts than it is through other means like reading large blocks of text, so having this organized is going to be one of the best ways to ensure that you are going to get some results in the process.

Make sure that when you are communicating the results that you get, that you spend some time adding in visuals, as well as some of the text document. This makes it easier for those who use the information to make key decisions to find the information that they want and to see what complex relationships are present, while also ensuring that they can see the methods and data that you used to come up with those visuals.

More is always better here, so the more that you are able to explain to those who need the information, the safer it is going to be. And make sure that this is done in laymen's terms as much as possible. This will ensure that you are able to get the complex relationships shared with the right people, without having to worry about them not understanding what is going on.

As we can see, there are a lot of different parts that have to come together in order to work with a data science project. Putting these all together and making sure that you understand what is going on, and how all of this is going to help your business to thrive will really be important to helping you to get some of the results that you would like and helping you to beat the competition in the process as well.

Chapter 5: How to Measure the Value of Our Big Data

One of the things that are really going to help drive some of the work that we will see with machine learning and data science is big data. This is going to be the data that we are able to use to drive our decisions and can help us to get some results and predictions from our algorithms over time. Big data is usually going to refer to the overabundance of information that we are able to collect in our modern world, but you will notice that it is not always about the amount of data that we have, and sometimes it is not even about the type of data we are working with. Often it is more about what we do with that data and the value that data can provide to us.

You can collect all of the data in the world that you want. But if you don't know how to use that data, and how to make it work for your needs, then it is going to be pretty much useless. Without knowing what information and patterns are found in the data, it is going to be really hard to use that data at all. You have to be able to use the right part of data science, and all of the different parts that come with this kind of analysis, in order to get the most out of this as well.

This is why we need to learn more about big data, and why it is so important to the process that we are trying to accomplish here. There are so many types of data, and so much of it, that we can easily fill up our storage areas in no time if we would like. But learning how to measure the value of this big data, and to figure out why this data can be so valuable to us, is important.

We don't want to just collect a bunch of random data and hope that it will be the right kind for our needs. Instead, we want to be able to collect the data that is actually right for us. We want to make sure that we are choosing the data that will be valuable to us, the data that is going to provide us with the best outcome for the business problems that we want to solve, and more.

Data itself is often going to be insignificant on its own. Measuring the value of the data we have is going to be a boundless kind of process that has a lot of approaches and options, whether you are working with structured or unstructured, and data is only going to prove to be as valuable as the business outcomes that it is going to make possible.

It is more about how we are willing to use that data that will allow us to really recognize the true value of it, and the potential to improve some of our own decision-making capabilities, and from a standpoint of business, measure it against the result of positive outcomes for the business.

The good news here is that there are many approaches to improving a decision-making process for a business, and to help us determine what the real value of our data is all about. This can include options like solutions, analytics sandboxes, intelligence systems for businesses, and data warehouses. Which one you choose is often going to be dependent on what results you are hoping to get in the process, and what kind of data you are working with as well.

These approaches are going to play a very high emphasis on how important each of the individual data items needs to that go into these systems. Because of this focus, it is going to highlight the importance of every single outcome that will link to a business and the impacts that it is able to deliver in the process as well.

Big data characteristics are often going to be defined through the four Vs including veracity, variety, velocity, and volume adapting these four options is going to provide us with a lot of different dimensions to the value of the data that we are working with at the time.

What Is Big Data

Big data is going to be a term that will describe the large volume of data, but the structured and the unstructured option, that will be able to help out a business on a day to day basis. But we have to remember that it is not going to be just the amount of data that is important. It is going to be what the company will do with all of that data they have been able to collect that is going to be the most important. We are able to take the big data and analyze it for insights, which are going to lead us to make better decisions and some of the best business moves based on our needs.

This brings us to the idea of why big data is going to be so important. The importance of this big data is not going to revolve around how much data you have, but what you would like to do with that data. You are able to take the data that you have from any source, and then analyze it a bit to find answers that can help you out in a few ways. You will find that these answers will help you to reduce costs, reduce the time it takes to do things, help with the development of some new products, and optimize the offerings that you give to customers, and ensure that you can make smart decisions as well.

When you are able to combine together big data with some analytics that are high-powered, you will be able to accomplish some of the tasks that are related to your business such as:

1. Determining the root causes of failures, defects, issues and more in near-real-time.
2. Working to recalculate the entirety of your risk portfolio in just a few minutes.
3. Generating coupons at the point of sale based on the buying habits of the customer.
4. Detecting some of the fraudulent behavior that might be going on before it is going to have a big effect on your organization.

We can then take a look at how this big data is going to work. Before we are able to discover the ways that big data is able to do for your business, you should first get a good understanding of where this data is going to come from in the first place. The sources that we will find for big data are generally going to fall into one of three categories.

The first one is streaming data. This is going to be the category that will include data that is able to reach your IT system from the web of devices that are connected and it is often going to be part of the IoT. You can analyze this kind of data as soon as it arrives and will then be able to make decisions on what data you would like to keep, what not to keep and what you need to for further analysis later on.

It is also possible for us to work with some of the data that comes with social media. The data on social interactions is going to be a really attractive set of information, particularly for the marketing that we see as well as the support functions and sales. It is often going to be in a form that is not labeled and pretty unstructured, so it is going to pose some unique challenges when it is time to consume and analyze this data.

And then we are going to find that we are able to get the data from some publicly available sources. Massive amounts of data are going to be really available through many open data sources. These can be a great way for you to make sure that you are able to find some more of the data that you need.

After you are able to identify some of the different sources that you are able to use for data, it is then time to consider some of the decisions that you will need to make once you begin harnessing the information. Some of the things that we need to consider when it is time for us to work with harnessing all of the data that we have is going to include:

1. How to manage and store the data: This used to be a big problem in the past. There are now some low-cost options to help you to store your data so that you are able to collect as much of it as you would like.

2. How much of the data you would like to analyze: There are a lot of options that you would like to work with depending on your overall goals. Some companies don't exclude any data out of the analysis, which is possible with some of the new technologies that are out there and some good computing and more. Another approach is going

to determine upfront which of the data is the most relevant before we go through and analyze it.

3. How to use the insights that you would like to uncover. The more knowledge that you are able to find and hold onto, the more confidence you are going to have in some of the decisions that you would like to work with. It is smart to have a strategy in place after you have been able to gather up an abundance of information and can sort through all of that.

The final step that we are able to work with when it comes to the idea of big data and making it work for your business is to research the technologies that will help you to make the most out of your big data and all of the analytics that you would like to work with. There are now a lot of the new technologies and more that we are able to work with when it is time to handle this data, and this makes it easier for us to work with this data and find out the information that is the most relevant to our business as well.

Basically, there is going to be an assumption that the data is going to be a lot of great potentials, but you have to actually go through that data in order to figure out what all of the potentials are going to be. Unlike what we are going to see with a traditional system of business intelligence, where an analyst is going to know what information they are seeking in the first place, the possibilities that come with exploring this big data are all going to be linked to some identifying connections between things that we don't really know. This all then becomes a process of designing a system to help decipher out this information.

One possible approach that we are able to use to figure out the value that we are going to be able to find with the big data we are using is to use the four Vs. When we bring these into focus and consideration, it will help us to determine what kind of value they are going to deliver, while still being able to solve the particular problem in the business that is bothering us.

So, with this in mind, how are we supposed to use those four Vs to help us determine the value of our big data and what we are going to be able to do with it overall? Some of the things to consider with each of them will include:

Volume Based Value

Now that most companies have the ability to go through and store as much data as they would like in a manner that is cost-effective, they are going to find that it is easier to do a broader analysis across a lot of different dimensions of the data, and also to do a deeper kind of analysis, going back through a ton of historical context and many years behind the data in order to come to the conclusions that they do.

What this means is that we will no longer need to go through and do a sampling of the data. We are instead able to carry out our whole analysis of the entire set of data. The scenario is going to apply heavily on developing true customer-centric profiles, and a lot of great offerings of the customer all the way to a micro-level.

The more data that a business is able to gather on their customer, both their recent customers and their historical customers, the greater the insights they will find. This is then going to turn to us generating better decisions around acquiring, retaining, increasing, and even managing the relationships that we are able to have with some of our customers.

Variety Value

Now that we have looked at some of the value that is going to come from having a good volume of data, it is time for us to explore why we can gather value when we have a lot of variety with the data that we are working with. There is a ton of variety that we are going to find when it is time to work with all of the data that is out there right now, which is going to be a great thing for you when completing data analysis.

In our current digital era, the capability to get ahold of and analyze all of this varied data is going to be really valuable. This is because many of the customers that your business is working with will be really diverse as well. And the more diverse your customer base is, and the more diverse the data about your customer you have, the broader the view is that you can develop around your customers.

When you are learning about your customers you do not want to know about just one or two points of the customer. You want to be able to go through and really learn as much as possible about your customers so that you can offer them the products they need, and you can market to them the right way. Having a good variety of data about your customers will make a big difference in the amount of success that you are able to have.

Being able to gather up a large variety of data is going to be able to provide you with some deep insights into successfully developing and then personalizing the customer journey maps, and provides a platform for a business to find themselves more engaged and aware of the expectations and needs of the customers.

Velocity Value

This one is going to take a look at some of the speed that happens with big data. You will find that the speed at which we are able to collect some of this big data is going to be so important right now, more than ever. The faster that a business is able to inject the data into their chosen algorithm or platform, the more time they are going to have to ask the right questions and to seek out the answers that they are looking for.

Rapid analysis capabilities are going to provide businesses with some of the right decisions in time to achieve their customer relationship management objectives. It is important to be able to gather up the information that is needed as quickly as possible and will ensure that we are able to see some of the best results with some of the algorithms and models that we want to work with.

Veracity Value

The next kind of value that we are going to take a look at is the idea of veracity While many questions the accuracy and quality of the data when we are looking at in the context of big data, but for innovative business offerings, the data accuracy is not that critical, at least when you are still in some of the beginner stages of validations and concept design. This means that the more that a business is able to churn out their hypotheses from all of the data they collect, the more potential they have to come up with an edge that will separate them out from the rest of the world as well.

Developing a framework of measurement taking these kinds of aspects into account will make it easier for a business to find a way to measure, in an easy manner, the value of data in their most important metric, and that is going to be the metric of money. Once implementing the platform that is needed for big data analytics, which measures along with the four Vs that we are looking for, it is then easier for the company to utilize, and then extend out, the outcomes to directly impact how they gather, onboard, retain, upsell, cross-sell, and more for their customers.

This is going to lead us to measure out the value of a parallel improvement on operational productivity and the influence of data across the enterprise of other initiatives.

Knowing how to work with the idea of big data and all of the different parts that it is going to entail will be so important. We need to make sure that we understand what big data is going to provide us with some of the information that is needed to really learn about the customer, learn about their industry, learn about the people and other companies in their industry and so much more. When we are able to put all of this together, it becomes so much easier for us to gain that competitive edge.

Chapter 6: Cleaning and Organizing Our Data

Data cleaning is going to be an important part of your data science project, but it is one that no one is going to spend that much time focusing on. It is not going to be the best or the sexiest part of machine learning, and there are not really all that many hidden tricks or secrets that you will be able to uncover to make this easier or add some fun to it.

Even without the glamour that is supposed to be there, doing the right kind of data cleaning is a good way to make or break the project that you are working with. Professionals in the world of data science are usually going to spend a large portion of their time on this step because it is so important. Why do they do this? Because it is always true to have better data rather than fancier algorithms that you get to work with.

What we are talking about here is that garbage is going to provide you with a lot of garbage out. even if you forget everything else in this kind of project, remember this point. You need to have strong and sturdy data in order to make sure that you get the best results out of the algorithm that you are doing. In fact, if you are able to properly clean out the set of data that you base your algorithms on, even simple algorithms are going to be impressive insights from all of that data.

One thing to remember with this is that the different types of data that you will use are going to require different types of cleaning. However, the systematic approach that we are working in this chapter is going to serve as a good place to start when it is time to handle the cleaning and the organizing of the data you have.

Remove the Observations That Are Not Wanted

The first thing that we need to focus on here is to make sure that we are getting rid of the unwanted observations that are in your set of data. This is going to include irrelevant or duplicate observations. The duplicate observations are mostly going to arise when you are working with data collection. They can happen when you receive any data from your clients or from other departments, when you scrape the data, or when you are taking more than one set of data from multiple places and combine them.

We also need to be careful about some of the observations that are pretty irrelevant. These are the ones that are not going to fit into the specific type of problem that you are working on. This doesn't mean that they are worthless observations, but they are just not pertinent to what you are doing now. For example, if you wanted to build up a model for single-family homes, you would not want to add in observations for apartments into the mix.

Fix the Structural Errors

The next thing that we need to take a look at is fixing all of the structural errors that are going on. Structural errors are going to be the ones that are going to show up when you are measuring the data when you are transferring the data or some of the other things that could fit into the idea of poor housekeeping.

For example, you can go through some of your data and then check to see whether there is something like inconsistent capitalization or typos. This is going to be a big concern for some of the categorical features, and you would then need to go through and look at the bar plot

that we can check. A good example of how this can work
is in the graph below:

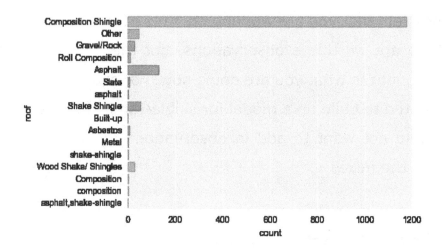

As you are able to see with this kind of graph, there are
going to be a few different things that you are going to
see is that there are a few options that you have to be
worried about. There are typos that show up, and the
capitalization is going to be off as well. After we have
been able to get through and replace some of the
inconsistencies that show up with the capitalization and
the typos, the class distribution that we are able to see
will show up better and become much cleaner overall.

And finally, in this part, we need to make sure that we
check out for some of the mislabeled classes. These are
going to be an issue that would include having separate

classes, even though these classes or these objects need to be the same. For example, if you have Not Applicable and N/A as two different classes, it is going to cause some issues because they should really be just one category that we should see.

Filter the Unwanted Outliers

The next thing that we need to look at is how to filter unwanted outliers. Outliers are going to cause us some problems with certain algorithms that we want to work with. For example, if we are working with the linear regression models, they are going to be less robust to outliers than some of the other models like decision tree models. For the most part, handling these outliers and making sure that they are not going to mess with the predictions and insights that you get will be important.

In general, if you can look at your outliers and you see that they are not that important, or you have another legitimate reason to remove an outlier, then it is something that you need to do right away. This is going to do so much to help out with the performance of your performance.

However, you will find that outliers are going to be innocent until they are proven guilty. Sometimes they are going to be useful for the work that you are doing and can provide you with some interesting information that will move you into the future and can provide you with a good idea of a new demographic to enter into, or something else that will improve your business. You should never take out an outlier because it is a big number if that is the only reason that you want to remove it. That big number could end up being really useful to the model that you would like to create.

It is important to always take a look at the outliers, and not just kick them out because this seems to be the most convenient way for you to handle some of these issues. You need to have a good reason to remove these outliers. If they are not going to work for some of your needs, or you see that they give you a suspicious kind of measurement that is going to mess with the rest of the algorithm, then it is best if you are able to avoid it.

Handle Any Missing Data

And we also need to take a look at what we want to do with handling some of our missing data. This is going to be an issue that can be deceptively tricky when you are working with machine learning. You want to be able to deal with it, but you are not able to just ignore the missing values that show up in any set of data that you have. it is important to handle these values in some way. This is because most algorithms are not going to accept these missing values at all because they don't like the idea of them and they can mess with the final results that you are going to get.

Of course, this gets harder to handle when we consider that common sense is not the best choice to go within this case. From experience in these algorithms and how they work, the two most commonly recommended ways of dealing with the missing data are not going to be a lot of fun and can take up a lot of your time and energy in the process. The two most common methods that you can use in order to handle some of the missing data before you send it through one of the algorithms will include:

1. Dropping the observations or the parts of your set of data that have missing values.
2. Input the missing values and you can use a number that is based on what you find with the other observations.

You will find that dropping the missing values is not usually the best option to go with. This is because when you drop some of the observations that you have, you are basically going to drop some of your information, and this is not usually a good thing when it comes to working with data science. You have to remember that the value that was missing could have been informative itself as well. And in the real world, it is possible that you will need to make predictions on some new data, even if some of the parts and the features that you would need to make these decisions on will be missing.

Imputing the missing values isn't always the best option either. This one does fill in the value that was missing for you, but you were the one who filled it in, rather than that information already being there and present for you to use. This is always going to end up with a loss of information, regardless of what kind of method you used in order to fix the problem.

Again, the missingness is almost always going to be in the information itself, and you should let the algorithm know, as much as possible, if one of the values was missing. Even if you build up a model that is able to add in some of these values for you, you are not adding in any real information. You are just going through and reinforcing some of the patterns that the other features were able to provide to you. This can make it a bit messy to work with, and may not provide you with some of the results that you want. Depending on how many missing values there are, it could end up really skewing the information and the predictions that you get.

No matter which method you are going to be using, it is important to tell your algorithm that value was missing because this is informative to the process as well. But the process of doing this can be tough, and it often depends on which kind of data is missing. You could miss out on categorical data, or on numeric data, and the method that you use in order to handle each of these will be a bit different.

When we are working with the categorical data, you will find that the best way to handle some of this missing data is to just put in a label and call it missing. You will essentially, with this option, be adding in a new class for the feature to handle some of this stuff. This is going to tell the algorithm that the value is missing but still lets it show up in the algorithm and be used. This is also going to help us get around the technical requirements that are in place that states we should not have any missing values.

And then we need to move on to handling the missing numeric data. For this kind of data, we need to flag and then fill in the values that we have. we can start with this by flagging the observation with an indicator variable. This is going to tell the system that something is missing because you don't have that information. Then you are able to go through and fill in the value that was missing originally with 0 just to meet some of the technical requirements of no missing values.

When you go through and use this technique of filling and flagging, you are basically going to tell the algorithm that it needs to estimate the optimal constant for the missingness, instead of just filling it in with the mean and hoping that it is all going to work out. this method is going to help us to really make sure that the predictions and the results that we get out of some of these algorithms are as accurate and helpful as possible, even if the values are missing and we are not sure how to fill them in.

The process of cleaning your data is going to be so important when it is time to handle some of your data. You do not want to just leave this information in its original form, because this is going to cause some issues with what you are able to see with the patterns and insights that come through. And in some cases, like with the missing values, the algorithm may not be able to handle that information at all. Being able to go through some of the steps that we have above and learn how to make this process take-off an organization the data more than ever, and ensures that you are able to get the nice patterns and insights that you need in the end.

Keep in mind that there are quite a few steps that go along with this though, and it is not always as easy as it is going to seem when you get started. many people do not realize how many steps go into the process of cleaning and organizing the data, and then they get frustrated when this is a process that takes them a long time and is not as easy to handle and work with as they had hoped.

This is a long process, and it can sometimes take longer to complete than any of the other stages. Don't let this frustrate you. The higher quality you can make your data before adding it to your algorithm for training and testing and using, the better. This is going to ensure that you are able to take care of the data and that it is going to work well with the different algorithms that you have. It may not be the most fun part of the data science process, but it is definitely one of the most important if you would like to work with data that is going to provide you with a solid base to make your decisions with.

Chapter 7: Your Guide to a Python Data Analysis

Another topic that we need to spend some time on here is known as data analysis. This is going to be similar to what we are going to see with a data science project, and in fact, it is one of the steps that come with data science as well. To start, data analysis is going to be the process of inspecting, cleansing, transforming, and then modeling the data that we have. And we are going to go through these steps with the idea of finding out more useful information, discovering some good conclusions, and to support our process of making decisions as well.

There are going to be a lot of approaches and facets that come with data analysis and many times you will be able to find a bunch of great techniques to help you get through this process. In many cases, the data analysis that we are using in statistics is going to be divided into three different parts including confirmatory data analysis, and exploratory data analysis, and descriptive statistics.

The data needs to be cleaned first, but we took some time in the past chapter to look at this. Then the data cleaning process is going to be where we are able to handle some of the outliers and other problems that show up in our data, to ensure that it is going to be perfect for the model that we want to work with. There are a few options when it is time to clean off your data, and the one that you are able to choose is going to depend highly on the type of data that you would like to clean.

For some of the quantitative data methods, the outlier detection can be used to make sure that we are kicking out some of those anomalies that may be in the data and mess with it. In addition, we could use something like a spell checker to make sure that there are no words that aren't spelled right that is messing with the data as well.

Business intelligence is often going to cover the type of data analysis that is going to run heavily on slicing and dicing and other types of processes and can focus on the business information. And then we can also work with predictive analytics which is going to be when we apply a structural or a statistical model for some of our predictive forecasting. Text analytics is the application of the structural, linguistic, and statistical models to help us to extract and then classify information from the texts.

Why are we looking at all of this? We are seeing all of the different varieties that you are able to pick from when it is time to complete your own data analysis. There are so many options that we are able to take a look at and learn from that it makes sense that we are going to spend some of our time learning how to work with these and learning what they are in the first place.

What Is Data Analysis?

As we mentioned before, there is a lot that is going to go into data analysis. There are different methods and techniques that we are able to work with, and you will find that when we are able to combine some of them together, and when we are able to pick out the right kind of algorithm to get the work done, there are a lot of great options that we are able to use to learn what is hidden inside all of that data.

Remember that the data analysis is going to be where we are able to clean, and organize the data, and then search through it to see what insights may be hidden within that information. You will find that there are a lot of parts that come with this, but it is basically the part where we get to finally bring out some of the algorithms that come with machine learning and deep learning and see what they are able to do.

This can be an exciting time because all of the other phases that you have gone through up to this point are going to come into use right now. You will be able to complete your data analysis and learn quite a bit out of all that information. You do have to go through the training and the testing phases first, but it is still something that is important for you because it is part of the fun of doing this type of project.

With the right algorithm in place and a nice set of data that is cleaned and organized, you are going to be able to gather up a lot of great predictions and insights. What you do with this information is going to depend on what your original goals were when you got started. But this is part of the main event that you have been waiting for this whole time!

Initial Phases of a Data Analysis

Now to start with this, we need to take some time to look at the initial phases that come with data analysis. The first phase is going to be known as data cleaning.

This is going to be the first process of data analysis and you are going to need to get to work. There are a lot of similarities that come here to the previous chapter, but you want to make sure that the data is as organized and clean as possible. In this phase, you are going to do things like column segmentation, deduplication, and record matching to make sure that the data that you collected from different sources are clean and ready to go.

From there, after we are sure that the data is clean and ready to go, it is time to work with something known as a quality analysis. Using a few tools like kurtosis, skewness, median, deviation, mean and more, you will find that we are able to go through and compare what is in the data with some of the external parts that we have on hand.

The point of going through and doing all of this is to make sure that the data we are using is higher in quality. If we are working with a data set that has a lot of bad values, or incorrect values, then we are going to end up with bad and inaccurate predictions and insights when we are all said and done with it. Of course, this is not what anyone wants, so it is important to double-check that the accuracy and the quality of your data are in place before you get started.

Then we need to make sure that we are working with a measurement tactic that is of higher quality. You do not want to go through all of that work of cleaning the data and making it look nice if you don't have a good algorithm or another good tool of measurement that you are able to use. You should pick out the algorithm that you want to use with as much caution as possible. This is going to be the thing that you push the data through and hopefully, make some good decisions based on, you want to make sure that it is good and accurate as well.

Then we need to move on to the actual analysis that we are working with. There are so many types of analysis that you are able to work with while you are working on the initial data analysis as well. This is going to depend on what you would like to find out of the data, and even what kind of data we are working with as well. Some of the options that we are able to work with here include:

1. Distribution
2. Continuous variables

3. Computation of some of the new variables you have

4. Exact tests or bootstrapping when we are working with smaller subgroups.

5. Loglinear analysis for helping us to identify important variables and some of the confounders that could possibly be there.

6. Hierarchical log-linear analysis

7. Associations

8. Frequency counts when we are working with percentages and numbers.

9. Ordinal and nominal variables.

10. Some of the different graphical techniques that you can use to see the data, such as the scatter plots

11. Bivariate associations correlations.

12. Single variable univariate statistics.

13. Box plots

14. Leaf and stem displays

15. And different parts of statistics like kurtosis, skewness, and even variance.

The Main Data Analysis

When you are done doing some of the initial analysis that we talked about before, it is time for us to move on to some of the main data analysis that we need to focus on. This is going to make it easier for us to dive into the data and really see what information is deep down inside of it. There are a number of steps that we will need to use in order to get this going and they will include:

You can start out with this process by using exploratory and confirmatory approaches. In the process that is known as an exploratory analysis, we will find that there is not going to be a clear hypothesis that is stated before we go through and analyze the data. Then we can also work with what is known as confirmatory analysis. This one is going to be a bit different because you will have a hypothesis, usually a pretty clear one, about the data that you are testing and you are going to use these to help you figure out whether or not they are true.

Another thing to consider when you are working with the main data analysis is some of the stability that you are able to see in the results. This is going to happen when you use a number of methods to check it out and make sure it all fits together. You can work with statistical methods, cross-validation, and sensitivity analysis to double-check.

Many times we think that we are going to just work with one type of statistical method in order to find the information that we need. This is a basic approach to the whole thing, but we need to make sure that we are understanding that often we need to work with one or two methods to help you really get through the data and learn what it is telling you. And sometimes, if you have a lot of data, you will find that working with more than two algorithms can be the answer that you need. There are a few different types of statistical methods that we are able to use to make all of this happen for our needs as well, and these will include:

1. General linear model: The first method that we are going to work with is known as a general linear model. These are going to be best on a lot of options like MANOVA< ANOVA, and more. This is going to be something that allows you to work with some generalizations when you have more than one dependent variable that you need to work with at the same time.

2. Generalized linear model: This is going to be one of the extensions, and even a generalization, of the model that we talked about. This is going to be used when we are working with some discrete dependent variables as well.

3. Structural equation modeling: The third option that we are able to work with is going to be structural equation modeling. These are going to be a good option to help us assess latent structures form measured manifest variables.

4. Item response theory: And the final option that we are going to need to take some time to look at is the item response theory. Models like this one are going to be used to help assess one latent variable away from several of the other binary measured variables that we are going to work with.

As we can see, there are a lot of different things that we need to work with when it is time to bring out the process of data analysis. This is a very important process when we are working with the data science project, and it is the fun part where we get to bring out the algorithms and see how well they are able to work on some of our data.

As we can imagine with this one, there are often going to be a lot of different options when it is time to pick out the algorithm that you would like to use. And each one, while it has a lot of benefits and a few drawbacks, will depend on what you are able to find in the data and what you are hoping to get out of it before you are able to jump on and see some of the results that you would like. Make sure to go through some of the steps that are above to make sure that you understand how to go through data analysis and use it for your own needs.

Chapter 8: Different Machine Learning Algorithms to Help with Data Science

Now that we know a little bit more about the process of machine learning and all of the other topics that are needed to help us handle some of our own data science project, it is time for us to move on and learn a bit more about some of the different algorithms that we are able to handle when it is time to work with this kind of process.

There are a number of different machine learning algorithms that we are able to work with and it often depends on the kind of data that we are able to work with, and what we are hoping to get out of the information in the first place. We are going to take a look at some of the different options that we are able to use when it is time to work with machine learning and Python, and how we are able to get these started in order to help with one of our own data analysis projects.

K-Nearest Neighbors Algorithm

The next algorithm that we are going to work with is the K-Nearest Neighbors algorithm or KNN. This one is going to be one that is a little different than other options that we will explore within this guidebook, and sometimes it is going to be seen as a more lazy approach because you have to actually ask it when you want a new prediction, rather than having it just do this automatically for you. If you would like the algorithm to wait to make new predictions anyway, then this is not such a big deal.

There are going to be some good benefits when you will work with the KNN algorithm. When you are about to work with this one, you are then able to use this to cut through the noise that comes with your set of data. This noise can be as loud as possible if you have a lot of data that you would like to work with, and getting rid of that noise is going to make a big difference in all of the information that you are able to get.

And any time that you would like to really work with a lot of data all at once, then the KNN algorithm is going to be a great option to choose. Unlike some of the others that are going to limit what you can sort through and may not be able to handle large amounts of data, the KNN algorithm is able to handle this whether the data amount is small or large.

Of course, we have to be careful with some of the computational costs that we are going to see this kind of algorithm. If you have a smaller project to work with or your budget for machine learning is lower, then this may not be the best option for you to work in the first place.

The good news is that the steps that you will need to use in order to get started with the KNN algorithm are pretty easy. The steps that you will be able to use for this one will include:

1. Load the data into the algorithm for it to read through.
2. Initialize the value that you are going to use and rely on for k.
3. When you are ready to get the predicted class, iteration from one to the total number of the data points that you use for training, you can use the following steps to help.
   a. Start by calculating the distance that is in between each of your test data, and each row of your training data. We are going to work with the Euclidean distance as our metric for distance since it's the most popular method. Some of the other metrics that you may choose to work with here include the cosine and Chebyshev.

b. Sort the calculated distances going in ascending order, based on their distance values.

c. Get the k rows from the sorted array.

d. Get the most frequent class for these rows.

e. Return back the class prediction.

K-Means Clustering

Clustering algorithms are going to be really good options to work with when it is time to handle some of the data that you would like with machine learning. Being able to work with a clustering algorithm is going to make a lot of difference in being able to see things more clearly. You may then be able to figure out how your industry is split up, the demographics of your customers, or something else that needs to be split up into several groups.

The idea that comes with these clusters is that all of the objects that are inside of one single cluster are going to be the ones that are the most closely related to one another. And then the ones that are outside of the same cluster will have fewer similarities to the items that are in some of the other clusters. This idea of similarity is going to be the metric that a business is able to work in order to reflect how strong the relationship is between the two objects of data.

One of the times when you are going to be able to use clustering, especially this kind of clustering, is going to be used with the process of data mining, especially if we are working with some kind that is more exploratory in nature. You could also use it in a lot of other processes like pattern recognition.

The algorithm is going to form some clusters of data that is based on how similar the data values are. You are then required to specify the value of K, which is the number of clusters that you expect the algorithm to make out of the data. The algorithm will start out by selecting a centroid value for each of these clusters. And then it is going to go through three steps in an iterative manner includes:

1. You will want to start with the Euclidian distance between each data instance and the centroids for all of the clusters.
2. Assign the instances of data to the cluster of centroid with the nearest distance possible.

3. Calculate the new centroid values, depending on the mean values of the coordinates of the data instances from the corresponding cluster.

It is also a good idea for us to take a look at some of the steps that we are able to use in order to find the k-means and ensure that we are able to work with some of the clusterings. And some of the different ways that you can implement the ideas that we have already talked about when it comes to machine learning. To help us learn how to do this, we are able to work with the soft k-means and how this will work inside of your code.

To ensure that we are able to do this kind of coding, we want to make sure that we are using some of the standard imports, and that we are able to set them up with the utility functions. This is going to be similar to what we see with the Euclidean distance, and then combine it with the cost function together. The formula that we are able to use to ensure that we are able to make this happen will include:

import numpy as np
import matplotlib.pyplot as plt

```
def d(u, v):
    diff = u - v
    return diff.dot(diff)



def cost(X, R, M):
    cost = 0
    for k in xrange(len(M)):
        for n in xrange(len(X)):
            cost += R[n,k]*d(M[k], X[n])
    return cost
```

After this part, we are going to take the time to define your function so that it is able to run the k-means algorithm before plotting the result. This is going to end up with a scatterplot where the color will represent how much of the membership is inside of a particular cluster. We would do that with the following code.

```
def plot_k_means(X, K, max_iter=20, beta=1.0):
    N, D = X.shape
    M = np.zeros((K, D))
    R = np.ones((N, K)) / K
```

```python
# initialize M to random
for k in xrange(K):
    M[k] = X[np.random.choice(N)]


grid_width = 5
grid_height = max_iter / grid_width
random_colors = np.random.random((K, 3))
plt.figure()


costs = np.zeros(max_iter)
for i in xrange(max_iter):
    # moved the plot inside the for loop
    colors = R.dot(random_colors)
    plt.subplot(grid_width, grid_height, i+1)
    plt.scatter(X[:,0], X[:,1], c=colors)


    # step 1: determine assignments / resposibilities
    # is this inefficient?
    for k in xrange(K):
        for n in xrange(N):
            R[n,k]  =  np.exp(-beta*d(M[k],  X[n]))  /
np.sum( np.exp(-beta*d(M[j], X[n])) for j in xrange(K) )


    # step 2: recalculate means
    for k in xrange(K):
```

```
        M[k] = R[:,k].dot(X) / R[:,k].sum()


    costs[i] = cost(X, R, M)
    if i > 0:
        if np.abs(costs[i] - costs[i-1]) < 10e-5:
            break


    plt.show()
```

One thing that you should notice here is that both the R and M parts are going to be seen as matrices. The R is going to be a matrix with this because it is able to hold onto 2 individual indices. In this case, those are going to be the k and the n. M is another matrix in this because it is going to contain the K individual and D-dimensional vectors that we are able to work with.

We can also look at the beta variable. This one is the part that is able to help us control how fuzzy, or how to spread out the membership of these clusters can be, and we can refer to this as the hyperparameters. From here, we are going to be able to create a main function that is responsible for making random clusters, and then we can call up the functions as we defined in the first place.

The code that we are able to use to get started with this includes:

```
def main():
    # assume 3 means
    D = 2 # so we can visualize it more easily
    s = 4 # separation so we can control how far apart the means are
    mu1 = np.array([0, 0])
    mu2 = np.array([s, s])
    mu3 = np.array([0, s])

    N = 900 # number of samples
    X = np.zeros((N, D))
    X[:300, :] = np.random.randn(300, D) + mu1
    X[300:600, :] = np.random.randn(300, D) + mu2
    X[600:, :] = np.random.randn(300, D) + mu3

    # what does it look like without clustering?
    plt.scatter(X[:,0], X[:,1])
    plt.show()

    K = 3 # luckily, we already know this
    plot_k_means(X, K)

    # K = 5 # what happens if we choose a "bad" K?
```

```
# plot_k_means(X, K, max_iter=30)


# K = 5 # what happens if we change beta?
# plot_k_means(X, K, max_iter=30, beta=0.3)



if __name__ == '__main__':
    main()
```

Random Forests

A random forest is going to be a bunch of decision trees that we are able to combine together. These random forests are going to be a popular option that will ensure that we are able to learn more about the various paths that we would like to take, and all of the possible outcomes that are going to come with these over time as well. There is a lot of potentials that will come with these random forests and help us to figure out a lot of problems.

For example, if you want to work with a ton of tasks that explore through all of the data, like dealing with missing values, or treating some of the outliers of the information that you have, then the random forest is going to help you get all of this figured out. it is one of the best algorithms to go with when you have some big decisions to make, and you need help figuring out which decision is the best one for you to work with as well.

Now, you will find that when it is time to handle a data analysis with machine learning, there will be a few times when you can bring out these random forests to help you get the work done. This is because the random forest is going to be one of the best ways to give you the results that you would like. And often they are able to complete the job, and do it better, than what you are going to see with some other algorithms. Some of the different methods and strategies that you are able to work with when it comes to these random forests, and that will help you work them in your way will include:

- When you are working on your own training sets, you will find that all of the objects that are inside a set will be generated randomly, and it can be replaced if your random tree things that this is necessary and better for your needs.
- If there are M input variable amounts, then m<M is going to be specified from the beginning, and it will be held as a constant. The reason that this is

so important because it means that each tree that you have is randomly picked from their own variable using M.

- The goal of each of your random trees will be to find the split that is the best for the variable m.

- As the tree grows, all of these trees are going to keep getting as big as they possibly can. Remember that these random trees are not going to prune themselves.

- The forest that is created from a random tree can be great because it is much better at predicting certain outcomes. It is able to do this for you because it will take all prediction from each of the trees that you create and then will be able to select the average for regression or the consensus that you get during classification.

Random forests are going to be a great tool for you to use when you want to bring out some data science with your machine learning, and there are a ton of advantages to working with the random forests rather than picking out some of the other algorithms that are out there. the first benefit is that the random forest is able to deal with both kinds of problems, whether they are regression or classification problems. Most of the other algorithms that you will work with only help with one or the other, rather than both of these problems.

Support Vector Machines

Another type of machine learning algorithm that we are able to use is going to be known as a support vector machine, or SVM. This algorithm is an option that the programmer is able to go with when they are working with problems that are either classifications or regressions, that are going to come up in some of the work that we are doing. This one is usually going to work with the classification problems that you have to handle, but can work well with other issues as well.

When you are working with this algorithm, in particular, you have to start by taking each of the items in your set of data, and then you must plot them so that they can turn into just one point on an n-dimensional space. N is going to basically be the number of features that you are planning on using with this process.

At this point, you will then need to take the value of all the features, and try to translate this to the value that is going to be in your coordinates. Once this part has been successful, it is time for you to determine what point will be your hyperplane. The hyperplane is the part that is going to be there to show you the differences between all of the classes that will show up.

Here we are going to notice that when we are working with the SVM, there will sometimes be more than one support vector that is going to show up on your chart. The good news is that many of these are just the coordinates that come with any individual observations that you come up with. You often will be able to find the best hyperplane without too much work. You will need to see the SVM as the frontier that is able to separate all of the observations into the proper classes, and that should leave you with two parts to focus on, the hyperplane and the line.

The first part of this that we need to spend time on is the hyperplane. As you go through with this one, it is possible that the algorithm is going to present you with more than one hyperplane that you will need to pick out from. This can be a challenge because you want to make sure that you are able to pick out the hyperplane that will direct your information properly, and will ensure that you make the best decisions. The good news is that no matter how many hyperplane options you end up with, there are a few steps that will help you to pick out the one that is right, and these will include:

- We are going to start out with three hyperplanes that we will call 1, 2, and 3. Then we are going to spend time figuring out which hyperplane is right so that we can classify the star and the circle.
- The good news is there is a pretty simple rule that you can follow so that it becomes easier to identify which hyperplane is the right one. The hyperplane that you want to go with will be the one that segregates your classes the best.
- That one was easy to work with, but in the next one, our hyperplanes of 1, 2, and 3 are all going through the classes and they segregate them in a manner that is similar. For example, all of the lines or these hyperplanes are going to run parallel with each other. From here you may find that it is hard to pick which hyperplane is the right one.
- For the issue that is above, we will need to use what is known as the margin. This is basically the distance that occurs between the hyperplane and the nearest data point from either of the two classes. Then you will be able to get some

numbers that can help you out. These numbers may be closer together, but they will point out which hyperplane is going to be the best.

The Markov Algorithm

Another option that we are able to take a look at is going to be the Markov Algorithm. This is going to be an algorithm that is going to take the data that you will be able to put some input into, and then the algorithm is able to translate it to help work in another coding language if you would like. One of the things that you are going to like about this process and what it is able to do for you is that it is going to be able to provide you with a way to set up your own rules with the algorithm and ensure that you are able to take the string of data that you would like and get it to be useful in figuring out any of the parameters that are needed for how the data is going to behave.

Another thing that you may like about this Markov algorithm is that you are able to work with it in several ways, rather than being stuck with just one method. One option to consider here is that this algorithm works well with things like DNA. For example, you could take the

DNA sequence of someone, and then use this algorithm to translate the information that is inside that sequence into some numerical values.

This can often make it easier for programmers, doctors, and scientists and more to know what information is present, and to make better predictions into the future. When you are working with programmers and computers, you will find that the numerical data is going to be much easier to sort through than other options of looking through DNA.

A good reason why you would need to use the Markov algorithm is that it is great at learning problems when you already know the input you want to use, but you are not sure about the parameters. This algorithm is going to be able to find insights that are inside of the information. In some cases, these insights are hidden and this makes it hard for the other algorithms we have discussed to find them.

There are still some downfalls to working with the Markov algorithm. This one can sometimes be difficult to work with because you do need to manually go through and create a new rule any time that you want to bring in a new programming language. If you only want to work with one type of programming language on your project, then this is not going to be a big deal. But many times your program will need to work with several different languages, and going in and making the new rules a bunch of times can get tedious.

The Naïve Bayes Algorithm

Another method that we are able to take a look at here is the Naïve Bayes. To help us figure out how this one is going to work, we need to be able to bring in our imagination a bit. Imagine for this one that you are working on a new project, and you want to handle a problem of classification. But you want to make sure that you are able to work with this project in order to come up with a new hypothesis that actually works. And at the same time, you would like to have a design so that you can add in a new feature and discussion based on the amount of importance that you want to place on each variable.

While this seems like something that is a lot of work, and like we are trying to fit in a ton of stuff in a short amount of time, it is something that we are able to get done.

Once you have spent your time gathering up the information and you are ready to go through some of the work that is needed with this algorithm, it is also likely that someone in the company is going to have some interest in knowing about the model and what you are hoping to produce.

They may even want to see it right from the beginning, and a long time before you are able to get the work done. This can present a dilemma. You want to make sure that you are presenting this in a manner that the other person, such as a stakeholder in the company, will be able to understand, but since the work is not done and you still have a lot to accomplish, it is hard to know how you will get this all done. How are you going to be able to show off all of this information to those who would like it without confusing them?

Many times when you are working with your data and creating a data analysis, you will end up having many thousands of data points, and it could have many more, and all of these need to show up in the model that you are working with. There are even some times when you would want to have some new variables that are going to help us to get the training and the testing done. How is it possible for us to show off all of this information to the shareholders in a way that they will be able to look it over and understand how it works, and still show off the information that you need.

The good news is that there is an algorithm that you can work with that will help you to stick with an early stage of the model that is easy to understand while you can still show all of the information that is needed. The algorithm that you will use for this is called the Naïve Bayes algorithm and it is a great way to use a few demonstrations to showcase your model, even when it is still at an earlier stage of development.

Let's take a look at how this is going to work with an example of apples. When you grab what is considered an average apple, you will easily be able to state that there are some distinguishing features that are present. This could include the fact that the apple is red, that it is round, and that it will be around three inches round. While these can sometimes be found in some other types of fruits, when all of these features are present together, then we know that the fruit in our hands is an apple. This is a basic way of thinking, but this is an example of working with the Naïve Bayes.

The Naïve Bayes model is a good one for us to work with because it is easy for us to pull together with our existing knowledge, and it is sometimes able to help us take a lot of data and turn it into a form that is simple and easy for us to understand. This is one of the biggest advantages that come with working on this model. It is simple, and easier to work with compared to the other models, and will ensure that you are able to fully understand the process that is going on.

As we can see, there are a ton of different algorithms that are out there that we are able to work with. Each of them will be able to handle the data that we have in a slightly different manner, but all of them can be effective when it is time for us to handle the data that we have and see some good results. Learn what data you would like to handle, and then work with the right algorithm to handle all of it as well.

Chapter 9: How to Handle Data Visualizations

The final topic that we are going to spend some time learning about in this guidebook is how we are able to handle some of our data visualizations. This is where we are going to be able to figure out the best way to present the data to those who need it the most. Often the data scientist and the person who is going to need to use the information for their own needs are not going to be the same people. A company will need to use that data in order to help them to make some good decisions, but they may not have the technical resources and knowledge in order to create the algorithms and get it all set up on their own.

This is why many times they are going to hire a specialist who is able to help them with the steps of the data science project. This is a great thing that ensures they are able to work with data in order to make some smart decisions along the way. but then the data scientist has to make sure that they are able to read the information. These algorithms can come out with some pretty technical information that is sometimes hard to understand if you do not know how to work with them.

This means that the data scientist has to be able to go through and find a way in order to share the information in a manner that the person who will use it is able to understand. There are a number of ways that we are able to do this, but we must remember that one of the best ways to do this is through the help of data visualization.

Sure, we can go through all of this and try to write it all up in a report or on a spreadsheet and how that this is going to work. And this is not a bad method to work with. But this is going to be boring and harder to read through. It takes a lot more time for us to read through this kind of information and hope that we are going to find what we need. It is possible, but it is not as easy.

For most people, working with a visual is going to be so much easier than trying to look through a lot of text. These visuals give us a way to just glance at some of the information and figure out what is there. When we are able to look at two parts of our data side by side in a chart or a graph, we are going to be able to see what information is there and make decisions on that a whole lot faster than we are able to do with just reading a few pages of comparisons on a text document.

Picking out the right kind of visual that you will want to work with is going to be so important to this process. You have to make sure that we are picking out a visual that works for the kind of data that you want to be able to show off to others. If you go with the wrong kind of graph, then you are going to end up with a ton of trouble. The visuals are important and can show us a lot of information, but they are not going to be all that helpful if you are not even able to read through them at all or if they don't showcase the information all that well in the first place.

Often when we take a look at a visual and all of the information that is there, we are going to be able to see a ton of information in a short amount of time. something that could take ten pages of a report could be done in a simple chart that takes a few minutes to glance at and understand. And when you are able to use a few of these visuals along the way, you are going to find that it is much easier to work with and understand what is there.

This doesn't mean that we can't work with some of the basics that are there with the reports and more. The person who is taking a look at the information and trying to make some smart decisions about it will find that it is really useful for them to see some of the backgrounds about your information as well. They need to be able to see how the data was collected, what sources were used, and more. And this is something that you are able to put inside of your data and text as well.

There is always a lot of use for a report of this kind, but we need to make sure that it is more of a backup to some of the other things that you have been able to do. If this is all that you have, then it is going to be really hard for you to work with some of this, and it can get boring to figure out what information is present in the data or what you learned about in your analysis.

The good news here is that there are a ton of different types of visuals that you are able to work with. This variety is going to help you to really see some good results with the data because you can make sure that you are able to find the visual that works for any kind of data that you are working with. There are options like histograms, pie charts, bar graphs, line graphs, scatterplots, and more.

Before you end your project, it is a good idea to figure out what kind of visuals you would like to work with. This is going to ensure that you are able to pick out the visual that will match with the data, and with the results, that you have gotten, and this will ensure that we are going to be able to really see the information that you need to sort through.

There are many options that you are able to work with as you need. You can choose to pick out the one that is the best for you, and maybe even try a few of these to figure out which one is going to pack the biggest punch and can help you to get things done. Make sure to check what your data is telling you, and learn a bit more about the different visuals that are there and how you are able to work with them.

With this in mind, we need to take a look at what is going to make good data visualization. These are going to be created when design, data science, and communication are able to come together. Data visuals, when they are done right, are going to offer us some key insights into data sets are that are more complicated, and they do this in a way that is more intuitive and meaningful than before. This is why they are often the best way to take a look at some of the more complicated ideas out there

In order to call something a good data visualization, you have to start out with data that is clean, complete, and well-sourced. Once the data is set up and ready to visualize, you need to pick the right chart to work with. This is sometimes a challenge to work with, but you will find that there are a variety of resources out there that you can choose to work with, and which will help you pick out the right chart type for your needs.

Once you have a chance to decide which of these charts is the best, it is time to go through and design, as well as customize, the visuals to the way that you would like. Remember that this simplicity is going to be key. You do not want to have so many elements in it that this distracts from the true message that you are trying to do within the visual in the first place.

There are many reasons why we would want to work with these data visuals in the first place. The number one reason is that it can help us to make some better decisions. Today, more than ever before, we are going to see that companies are using data tools and visuals in order to ask better questions and to make some better decisions some of the emerging computer technologies, and other software programs have made it easier to learn as much as possible about your company, and this can help us to make some better decisions that are driven by data.

The strong emphasis that there is right now on performance metrics, KPIs, and data dashboards is easily able to show us some of the importance that comes with monitoring and measuring the company data. Common quantitative information measured by businesses will include the product or units sold, the amount of revenue that is done each quarter, the expenses of the department, the statistics on the employees, the market share of the company and more.

These are also going to help us out with some meaningful storytelling as well. These visuals are going to be a very big tool for the mainstream media as well. Data journalism is already something that is on the rise, and many journalists are going to rely on really good visual tools in order to make it easier to tell their stories, no matter where they are in the world. And many of the biggest and most well-known institutions are already embracing all of this and using these visuals on a regular basis.

You will also find that marketers are going to be able to benefit from these visuals. Marketers are going to benefit from the combination of quality data and some emotional storytelling that is going on as well. Some of the best marketers out there are able to make decisions that are driven by data each day, but then they have to switch things around and use a different approach with their customers.

The customer doesn't want to be treated like they are dumb, but they also don't want to have all of the data and facts are thrown out at them all of the time. this is why a marketer needs to be able to reach the customer both intelligently as well as emotionally. Data visuals are going to make it easier for marketers to share their message with statistics, as well as with the heart.

Those are just a few of the examples of how we are able to work with the idea of data visuals for your needs. There are so many times when we are able to complete a data visually, and then use it along with some of the other work that we have been doing with data analysis to ensure that it provides us with some more context on what is going on with our work.

Being able to not only read but to understand, these data visuals has become a necessary requirement for this modern business world. because these tools and the resources that come with them are readily available now, it is true that even professionals who are non-technical need to be able to look through this data and figure out some of the data that is there.

Increasing the literacy of data for many professionals, no matter what their role in the company is all about, is going to be a very big mission to undertake from the very beginning. This is something that your company needs to learn how to focus on because it is really going to end up benefiting everyone who is involved in the process as well. With the right kind of data education and some good support, we are going to make sure that everyone not only can read this information, but that they are more informed, and that they are able to read the data and use that data to help them make some good decisions overall. All of this can be done simply by being able to read through these visuals.

Conclusion

Thank you for making it through to the end of *Python for Data Science*, let's hope it was informative and able to provide you with all of the tools you need to achieve your goals whatever they may be.

The next step is to be to put all of the different topics that we have discussed in this guidebook to good use and make sure that you are able to complete your own data science project with the use of Python. There are a lot of different parts that come together when it is time to work with a data science project, but it is important for us to spend some time looking for the best way to get started for your needs.

This guidebook has spent some time taking a look at the best steps that you are able to take in order to see some good results with a data science project for your own needs. We looked a bit more at what artificial intelligence is all about, how to work with machine learning and deep learning, and even what data science is going to entail as well.

From there we moved on to how to clean and organize our data, why big data is important to make sure that this process is going to work for our needs, and some of the different parts that come with data analysis, the algorithms that you can write with the help of Python and machine learning, and how to work with some data visualizations as well. There is so much that we are able to do with data science, and so many benefits that it can bring to your business, that it makes sense to learn all of the different aspects that come with it to use for some of your own needs as well.

When you are ready to learn a bit more about data analysis and completing your own data science project with the help of the Python language, make sure to check out this guidebook to help you get started.

Finally, if you found this book useful in any way, a review on Amazon is always appreciated!

www.ingramcontent.com/pod-product-compliance
Lightning Source LLC
Chambersburg PA
CBHW071133050326
40690CB00008B/1448